Understanding *Emotions* in the Classroom:

Differentiating Teaching Strategies for Optimal Learning

Claudia Marshall Shelton
&
Robin Stern, Ph.D.

DUDE PUBLISHING
A Division of
National Professional Resources, Inc.
Port Chester, New York

Library of Congress Cataloging-in-Publication Data
Shelton, Claudia Marshall
    Understanding emotions in the classroom :
differentiating teaching strategies for optimal learning/
Claudia Marshall Shelton & Robin Stern.
      p.cm.
      Includes bibliographical references.
      ISBN 1-887943-65-X

      1. Learning, Psychology of. 2. Teaching--
Psychological aspects. 3. Classroom management.
4. Emotions. 5. School environment--Psychological aspects.
6. Students--Psychology. 7. Teachers--Training of.
I. Stern, Robin. II. Title.

LB1060.S54 2003   370.15'23
                          QBI33-1591

Cover/Book Design & Production by Andrea Cerone, National Professional Resources, Inc.,
Port Chester, NY

Dude Publishing
A Division of National Professional Resources, Inc.
25 South Regent Street
Port Chester, New York 10573
Toll free: (800) 453-7461
Phone: (914) 937-8879

Visit our web site: www.nprinc.com

Printed in the United States of America

ISBN 1-887943-65-X

#53942194

To Those Who Teach and Guide the Development of Self-Awareness
In Children Throughout the World;

And to Our Children Who Lead Us to Develop Our Own Self-Awareness,
Christopher and Ryan Shelton; and Scott and Melissa Stern Mannis;

And to Our Mothers and Fathers Who Led Us to This Path,
Ellen and Rudolph Marshall; and Rosalind and David Stern.

Contents

Emotional awareness can influence students' learning behavior
and teachers' understanding of their classroom. Perspective
on the emotional brain. Definition of terms. Framework on
developing self-awareness from K-12. Overview of the book.

Model for identifying and defining opportunities for teaching
self-awareness in all classes. Importance of specific terms
to increase student understanding. Questions for teachers to
consider how their own self-awareness informs their teaching.

System for teachers, students and parents to understand how
emotion is more central to the learning of some students than
others. Teaching students to be aware of their own learning
dynamics, and contract to build complementary skills.

A classroom where students gain awareness of differing
emotional reactions to the same event, and identify varying
levels of intensity of the same emotion. How this learning influences classroom cooperation and attitude toward learning.

A school where basic skills in emotional awareness are taught
in all K-5 classrooms, and integrated with counseling, professional development and discipline programs—increasing
learning effectiveness, school climate and staff morale.

Foreword

For more than three decades now, I have worked in the field of public education in many capacities including as a classroom teacher, school administrator, and director of one of our country's largest school programs in social and emotional learning—the Resolving Conflict Creatively Program (RCCP) of Educators for Social Responsibility. The one theme that has followed me throughout my career is what this book so eloquently advocates: when we nurture our inner lives and develop skills of self-awareness, it not only enhances our own teaching process, but also helps children perform more successfully in school and in life.

Self-awareness can be the first step in helping children to understand and manage the important role emotion plays in their intellectual development. Children who lack it are often unaware of their feelings. With their feelings blocked, less capacity is available to children to process what they are to learn intellectually. If these blocked feelings are ignored over time, there is more potential for choosing risky, unhealthy behaviors such as violence, social withdrawal, and drug use. Fortunately, by developing the skills of self-awareness, children can often turn this situation around. They can develop the decision-making skills that enable them to understand their feelings and make constructive choices for themselves.

As we struggle to live productively in a world of ongoing terrorism, poverty, and racial and religious hatred, many of us are aware of how we hold in our individual and collective hands the opportunity to use our inner and outer lives to advance either unbearable evil, devastation, and moral breakdown or to promote goodness, transformation, and hope. However, educators who believe in the value of self awareness and emotional learning as a developmental discipline have a better chance of creating the necessary climate for helping students to understand and manage their responses. Claudia Shelton and Robin Stern inspire us to create "self-aware schools" where educators nurture the kind of self-knowledge and insight necessary to tackle the deep academic, emotional, social, political, and ethical dilemmas of our time.

Understanding Emotions in the Classroom challenges us to make all of our classrooms places where there is a special understanding of the needs of all learners, and a high degree of emotional safety where children and teachers know how to identify, manage, and understand their feelings and perceptions. The authors encourage us to do this inner work together.

If you want to create more "self-aware" classrooms for yourself and your children, this book has a wealth of concrete "how-to" examples. It offers a solid framework for developing self-awareness skills across academic subjects, as well as integrating them into the curriculum at each grade level K-12. It is filled with inspirational stories of real teachers who care about schools as places that welcome attentive, reflective and emotionally skilled learners.

Sally Hare, teacher, educator and director of the Center for Education and Community, sums up what Shelton and Stern advocate for when she defines the "reflective practitioner" as:

> Those who can, *do*
> Those who can *reflect* and *understand* how to do
> Can *teach* others to *do.*

Understanding Emotions in the Classroom is written by two gifted friends and colleagues, who are insightful and emotionally reflective practitioners. They "can teach others to do" because they are powerful models of this work themselves. Shelton and Stern have done a remarkable job of inspiring us to embrace these capacities ourselves so that we might more authentically offer it to our children. As I look at the huge problems our young people will inherit in responding to violence, terrorism and unrest throughout our world, I can't imagine how we will make it without inner wisdom and guidance. My hope is that we each take up the challenge Claudia Shelton and Robin Stern advocate for building more "Self-Aware Schools."

Linda Lantieri
Director,
New York Office of the Collaborative for Academic,
Social, and Emotional Learning (CASEL)

Gratitudes

Many people have contributed in important ways to the development of this book. We are deeply grateful to our friend and colleague Fred Stern for his unflagging commitment to emotional education, and for joining us in the early teaching of emotional awareness to educators.

Those who supported the birthing of the book through discussion and perceptive feedback include Gemma Baker, Claire Carter, Kay Clarke, Kaye Delano, Joyce Humphrey, Muffie Knight, Pam Morgan, Marilyn Nemarich and Mimi Stepp. John O'Neil at ASCD recognized the seeds of this book in earlier published articles. Laila Kain brought a sensitive writer's eye to the foundation of the first chapters.

At formative stages of our own thinking, many colleagues provided insight. Jack Wideman and Janine Roberts at the University of Massachusetts and the late Philip Merrifield of New York University helped each of us define our own perspectives for looking at self. Other psychiatrists, psychologists and psychotherapists, including Madeline Berley, Andy Cohen, Jon Cohen, Arthur Gray, Frank Lachman, Les Lenoff, Marty Livingston, Richard Meyer and Many Shapiro, contributed to the understanding of the role of self-awareness in a healthy life perspective.

Conversations with Jennifer Allen, Robin Bernstein, Rachel Brod, Kate Cannon, Janet Patti, Ted Repa and Michele Seligson brought insight about the importance of self-awareness to personal development. Naomi Wolf, at The Woodhull Institute for Ethical Leadership, brought additional perspective about the relationship of self-awareness to professional development.

Colleagues in the field of social and emotional education, including Linda Bruene, Maurice Elias, and Linda Lantieri, provided a foundation for how we approach this work with educators. Sandra Seagal and David Horne, Janet Levine and Alice Ray provided creative thinking and guidance for how to bring the complex process of self-awareness into the classroom effectively. A special thanks is offered to Daniel Goleman for his groundbreaking work and inspiration in focusing public attention on the importance of emotional intelligence in American education.

Many teachers, school principals and counselors have encouraged the development of the actual school applications. We are grateful especially to Jane Shipp, Margaret Ayres and Gladys MacDonough of Renbrook School; Angela Murphy from the Community School of Naples; Vicky Poedubicky from Bartle School; Jonathan Gray and Melissa Moskowitz at the School of the Future; Marjorie Robbins, Barbara Luque,

Sheila Brown and Jim Tobin from Project EXSEL in Manhattan District 2; and Jack Dexter, Jim Best, Lisa Alberti and Lindsay Obrig at Trevor Day School. We thank Donna Klein, Karen Mildener, Pat Hunter and Christie Riccio, who piloted early work in the classroom. We want to recognize all of those other administrators, counselors and teachers who have conducted the work in their own classrooms, and whose names will be identified in specific chapters throughout the book.

The book could not have been completed without the early insights of editors Bob Cole and Ernesto Yermoli. Special thanks also go to our research assistant Lori Ramsey who brought critical thinking and insight as well as tireless editorial support.

Bob and Helene Hanson, our publishers, brought their unique understanding of the importance of emotional education and learning in a way that added depth to our work. We particularly value their perspective as experienced educators. We are also grateful for the talented contributions of graphic designer, Andrea Cerone, and co-editor, Lisa Hanson, to the final development of the book, as it appears today.

Finally we give thanks to our partners, Jim Shelton and Frank Moretti and our families, who provided personal support, time and the space necessary to complete this project as we put many day-to-day priorities on hold. Without their understanding and flexibility, the project would not have been possible.

To all these people and to the many others who supported us through the work, we are truly grateful.

Introduction:
Leave No Child Behind

Emotions are central to classroom learning. Strong emotions compel our attention. Unexpressed emotions can lead to irritation and distraction. Emotional connection to a subject can be a powerful motivator for performance. Conflicting emotions can prevent us from being able to pay close attention to our work. Remember some of your best and worst moments in the classroom. Chances are these moments elicit emotional reactions from you even now.

We are deeply committed to understanding the influence of emotional self-awareness on classroom teaching and learning. We want our readers to recognize the opportunity that comes from developing this awareness and building emotional competence in themselves and their students. The results, we believe, can increase classroom performance, and strengthen the resilience and vitality of teachers and students alike.

In writing the book, we built upon one another's experience: Claudia's as a school counselor, teacher, administrator and leadership specialist, Robin's as a psychotherapist, educator, and specialist in emotional intelligence and leadership development. We reached out to other professionals whose work we have tried and respect, and have included some of their methods. We also interviewed many teachers, administrators and school counselors, and share their successful stories.

The book speaks in three voices: sometimes we speak as one; other times we come primarily from an individual perspective. Several of the Chapters represent our shared voices, including the overview of this educational arena in Chapter 1 and related professional development activities in Chapters 12 and 13. Claudia's experience from the classroom voices itself in Chapters 2, 3, 6, 7, and 9. Robin shares her experience in university teaching and school consulting in Chapters 10 and 11. Chapters 4 and 5 reveal our individual observations of well-known and researched programs at schools we visited. Claudia offers administrative perspective in the roadmap of Chapter 14. All of this has been reviewed through numerous discussions, drafts and revisions. What we offer is an integrated, developmentally-sound, instructional approach to building performance-oriented self-awareness in both teachers and their students.

Clearly, every student has an individual emotional make-up. Students' self-awareness and understanding of the reflective process is the first step to helping them manage the role that emotion plays in their learning process. The better able students are to turn inward and recognize emotional patterns that occur as they sit in the classroom, study, take tests, encounter distractions and socialize with others, the more effective they become in managing these activities. The earlier students develop self-awareness and self-management strategies, the more integral these tools become to effective learning. In addition, these strategies offer teachers ways to increase motivation, decrease anxiety and stress, increase methods for problem-solving about performance blocks, and develop a stronger sense of well-being and morale—in spite of the increased pressures.

As educators respond to the national goal to "leave no child behind", we believe that building self-awareness can play a vital and integral role in individualizing your school's approach to higher performance standards. The professional development opportunities presented throughout the book can reinforce many components of your Title I programs, including building technology education, parent involvement and parent literacy, drug and violence prevention, and character education. The central message of the book speaks to Title 2 goals of providing professional development for improving classroom behavior and teaching children with different learning styles.

Finally, we believe that effective, performance-oriented teaching always begins with one motivated and effective teacher. Therefore, the book is designed for one teacher working alone in the classroom. However, we also offer guidance to expand the approach for a group of teachers across the curriculum, or even the total faculty of a school or district. Many of the teachers who have attended our classes and workshops are, in fact, the trailblazers who see the value of this work, and bring it back to their colleagues. We have titled the concluding chapter of the book, *It All Starts with a Teacher!*, and that is the thought we want you to keep in mind as you begin reading Chapter 1.

1
Understanding Emotion Builds Learning and Teaching Power

As teachers, we are usually focused on the "thinking levels" of our classrooms—how we analyze, organize, problem-solve and discuss lessons. Yet in every classroom, emotions are constantly at work within both students and teachers. Many of us have learned to ignore these feelings and focus on the important lessons of our busy class schedules. However, recent brain research suggests that if we better understand the "emotional information" conveyed by our emotions and feelings, we can increase the effectiveness of our teaching and our students' learning.

In ***Understanding Emotions in the Classroom***, we invite you to explore 1) how the experience of emotions and feelings can influence teaching and learning; 2) the powerful influence of self-awareness—and particularly emotional awareness—on both teacher and student classroom behavior; and 3) the central role that a teacher's own self-awareness plays in guiding the emotional experience of the classroom. In essence, students learn best to understand how their own emotions influence learning from teachers who effectively model and practice emotional self-awareness.

In addition, as teachers become more self-aware, they are usually better able to be non-judgemental in understanding and responding to learning differences among students—an essential competency for differentiating classroom instruction. As one teacher succinctly expressed it: "You can't effectively teach in a differentiated classroom without constant awareness of the differences in learning processes among teacher and students."

The Power of Self-Awareness on Learning Performance

Self-awareness is the process of focusing attention on one's thoughts, feelings, and behaviors in order to understand what they are, where they come from, and what they mean. The self-aware person knows that feelings are different than thoughts and actions. As we become more self-aware, we gain a clearer sense of ourselves, which we can then use to determine our actions. The result of this reflective process is *self-knowledge*—the ultimate gift we can give to ourselves to maximize our ability to make conscious choices.

As renowned author Daniel Goleman (1995, p.47) points out in *Emotional Intelligence*, "Self-awareness is not an attention that gets carried away by emotions, over-reacting and amplifying what is perceived. Rather, it is a *neutral mode* that maintains self-reflectedness even amidst turbulent emotions." *Self-awareness is not simply the experience of recognizing our thoughts and feelings. It involves being able to self-observe those thoughts and feelings without judgment in a way that allows us to understand them and consciously make independent decisions about how to act on them.*

Consider a common everyday experience: We decide to diet to lose weight, and set up a rational approach to weight loss with all kinds of rewards built in for reaching interim goals. This well thought out cognitive strategy works effectively, right? Well, what happens when we experience the feeling of wanting that candy bar? Can we find that neutral mode of self-awareness to recognize our "candy questing" feeling, understand the strength of that feeling, yet remember our own best strategy for impulse control so that we make a deliberate decision to ignore the candy bar? Or do we confuse our thoughts and feelings, get carried away by emotion, and choose not to think about how personally challenged we are by the temptation and gulp the candy? Self-awareness is critical to finding that place within ourselves from which we can choose our diet plan. As we will soon see, it is also a critical skill in understanding student capacities for learning, and our own effectiveness in teaching.

The development of self-awareness is linked to school performance. Psychologist Maurice Elias (Elias, Tobias, & Friedlander, 1999) explains that children who lack self-awareness are unaware of their feelings and therefore find it difficult to control impulsive actions, make appropriate decisions, and communicate what they mean. Because these abilities help children to listen attentively, attend to their work consistently, and find constructive ways of overcoming setbacks, they are essential to academic achievement. Children cannot learn to read or do math unless they can focus attention on the subject. Emotion can literally overwhelm concentration (Goleman, 1995, p. 79) as "working memory" becomes swamped and is literally unavailable to hold in mind additional information required to complete a task. Fortunately, by learning many of the skills offered in this book, students can again find within themselves the neutral mode from which to think clearly.

Self-awareness also helps already strong students to excel even more. Self-aware children understand how to "read" a classroom situation, articulate their feelings and ideas, and concentrate and follow through on their plans. For example, consider a child who is unable to understand a class presentation, and begins to ask questions which the teacher ignores. The student may initially feel that the teacher doesn't like her, and want to withdraw. The self-aware child will experience and respect her feeling but will have the perspective to consider that feeling as input to problem solve. She might then recognize that the teacher is not explaining the subject in a way she can understand, and approach the teacher after class for help. She might also approach a student, who appears knowledgeable in class, to get advice.

In contrast, the unaware child might stop at the point of feeling disliked by the teacher and stay trapped in believing that feeling disliked is sufficient reason for poor performance. This child is unable to differentiate between feelings, thoughts and behavior, and thus is unable to use self-knowledge to make constructive choices. Such behavior will likely inhibit the child's problem solving ability and continue a self-defeating cycle.

A study conducted by psychologist Walter Mischel (Goleman, 1995) shows the long-term impact of impulse control and demonstrates important insights about self-awareness in the early stages of learning. Mischel posed the following challenge individually to four-year-olds: if they could delay eating a marshmallow placed directly in front of them for 15 to 20 minutes when left unsupervised, they would get two marshmallows when the researcher returned. A hidden video camera captured the many ways children resisted the marshmallow—by talking to it, sniffing it, and making gestures to it. When researchers revisited the children 12 to 14 years later, they found that those who had been able to delay eating the marshmallow were remarkably different from their marshmallow-gobbling counterparts. As a group, the delayed marshmallow eaters were more academically competent and scored an average of 210 points higher on their SAT scores. The group also scored higher on a range of social and emotional competencies.

We believe the research reveals that there is something that goes on between feeling and action that begins to develop (or not develop) in the very early years of a child's life. The delayed-marshmallow-eating four-year-olds demonstrate that when they feel a certain way, they can create coping techniques to manage themselves. Within the group of children who did not eat the marshmallow, there was an intervening process, which we believe indicates early skills in self-awareness. The delayed-marshmallow-eaters had learned to access this neutral mode.

The relationship between self-awareness and academic achievement appears to continue in the transition from high school to college, according to research conducted with first year college students by James Parker (2001) at Trent University. Parker's results suggest that intra-personal skills are one indicator of students with higher academic performance in college. Self-awareness is a crucial ingredient in both developing successful strategies for managing one's studies as well as building effective interpersonal relationships in the context of learning.

Brain and Behavioral Research Clarifies the Role of Emotion in Learning

Until very recently, those who studied the brain believed that it was governed by a hierarchy of functions, at the top of which was cognitive thinking. The emotional brain was not known to exist, and emotion itself was regarded as a lower level function rather than as a vital, contributing element in the development of critical thinking. Emotions, feelings, and emotional information were seen as distractions from the educational focus; the role of emotion was considered peripheral to the learning experience. When emotion was discussed, it was predominantly in the context of problems such as drugs, alcoholism, anorexia, suicide, conflict, and abuse. This learning paradigm assumed that the rational information of the cognitive brain was paramount to the development of appropriate decision-making abilities among students.

We now know from a biological perspective that emotions are integral to the learning process. Brain research (Damasio, 1999) has identified the existence of an emotional brain and suggests that the constant interaction of the experience of emotion, with its simultaneous impact on the body and other parts of the brain, leads to the individual's interpretation of feelings. The emotional brain is a partner with the cognitive brain in the learning experience. The brain operates, therefore, not as a hierarchy but as a cooperative. For example, while the cognitive brain devotes its time to sifting through words, concepts, and analyses, the emotional brain discerns meaning and judgment from subtle nuances in voice tone, gesture, or eye contact. Studies by Albert Mehrabian (Cooper & Sawaf, 1996) show that unless speakers are highly believable, ninety-three percent of listeners will pass judgment based on voice tone and body language as processed by the emotional brain.

Translating this to the classroom, teachers may believe they are objectively evaluating a student's words, concepts and analyses; however, a student's voice tone, gesture, and eye contact will simultaneously influence the teacher's evaluation as the teacher's brain processes the total experience of the student. The same will be true for the student's experience of the teacher and of other students. We simply cannot separate the actual experience of our cognitive and emotional learning processes. However, through self-awareness we can find a way to observe and clarify our responses to the teaching and learning experience.

Recent behavioral studies have also emphasized the importance and integral role of social-emotional learning. For example, the New Haven Social Development Project (1990) demonstrated how increased social and emotional skills of students result in improvements in their attitudes about school, feelings of school safety, retention rates and progression to college. A two year evaluation of the Resolving Conflict Creatively Program, which will be discussed in greater detail in Chapter 4, found that, "students in the program tended to be less hostile, less likely to resort to aggression, and more likely to choose verbal rather than physical strategies to resolve conflict" (New York Times, 1999).

Teaching and Learning Self-Awareness

Self-awareness begins in early childhood, as children gradually develop their reflective capabilities and learn to process emotional information. Consider the following examples:

- A three-year-old grabs a toy from another child, and you give her a "time out"—in other words, you remove the child from the situation and encourage her to use the time to think about what she has done.
- A five-year-old comes back from art class and you ask him what aspect of the class he enjoyed the most. He says, "When I put my fingers in the finger paints and it felt cool." This child recognizes that feelings can arise from body sensations.
- A seven-year-old comes back from gym and you say, "Boy, you look very upset. What happened?" She says, "I'm really mad at the gym teacher. She wouldn't let me be on the team with my friend." This student has learned to identify not only her feeling but also the problem underlying this feeling, which is not always easy for children.

Children continue to develop self-awareness skills as they grow older (see Exhibit 1.1 at the end of this chapter). For example, a self-aware 10-year-old might be completely furious and yet understand that she isn't going to hit her friend just because she feels like it. She has learned to distinguish between her feelings and the appropriate way to act on them. Similarly, a 15-year-old may feel badly about saying "no" to an offer of marijuana from a friend, but nevertheless does so because he believes refusing the drug is in his best interest; he is able, in other words, to identify and sort through his "mixed feelings." If students are unaware of their feelings when pressured to take drugs, they may not be able to distinguish the possible excitement and the fear of the drug from a desire to belong to the group. Similarly, children who believe it's okay to hit a friend in anger haven't learned to distinguish between their feelings and appropriate actions.

Self-awareness skills develop as children learn to identify, describe, and respond to feelings, and to understand that feelings are often various and conflicting. If students practice self-awareness in their daily learning, they can develop the capacity to incorporate self-knowledge about their feelings into their everyday decisions. Every social and emotional skill is built on self-awareness: children cannot effectively manage their thoughts and behaviors or effectively relate to others unless they are knowledgeable about themselves.

The good news is that self-awareness can be learned at a very early age; the bad news is that many adults have never been taught self-awareness skills themselves. If parents are not self-aware, they cannot impart the requisite skills to their children. In this case, a cyclical pattern of emotional ignorance, self-denial, delusion, and deception is passed on from adult to child and back again, leading to frustration, timidity, insecurity, and even depression.

Well-meaning parents and teachers can sometimes unwittingly invalidate the reflective experience of kids. For example, let's say a student comes back from lunch and says, "I'm starving," and you respond, "No, you're not. You just ate!" This reply is a *self-awareness buster,* invalidating the child's description of his feelings. A *self-awareness booster,* on the other hand, reinforces self-awareness: "You're hungry. Wow! You must be growing. We can't eat again now, but snack is coming in 30 minutes. Tell your stomach to be patient." Exhibit 1.2, at the end of this chapter, offers additional examples of statements that either boost or bust self-awareness.

Of course, self-awareness does not mean permissiveness; we can acknowledge children's feelings without agreeing with their conclusions. But unless we recognize their feelings, and go the extra step of validating their feelings aloud, we teach them not to trust their inner emotional information.

You can reinforce your students' self-awareness by encouraging self-reflection. For example:

- State out loud that you value your own and your students' inner information and self-knowledge. Let students know that you WANT to hear from them regarding what they think and feel.
- Acknowledge self-aware language and expression of emotion

whether you agree with it or not. This will serve to reinforce students' skills.
- Consistently model self-reflective statements out loud. For example, you might say: " Gosh, I feel butterflies in my stomach! The school election is really important to so many of you. I am so anxious to know the winner. Let's go down and hear the results!"
- Talk about other people's self-reflection. You might say: " I heard Ms. Simms talking about how frustrated she is that she loses her umbrellas each year…so much so that when I got to school this morning I heard her using self-talk to calm herself down just because it is raining!!"
- Use techniques and visual aids such as those presented in this book to help kids turn their attention inward for information and reference points.

The self-reflective process that leads to self-awareness can be either momentary, focusing on a particular instance or emotional event, or can be part of an integration of impressions occurring over a period of time. As the examples in Exhibit.1.3 (at the end of this chapter) illustrate, we develop self-awareness by understanding the ways in which we encounter the world and reflect on our inner understanding of such experiences. The result of this crystallization of mindfulness and experience is self-knowledge.

Stop and think for a moment about the evolution of your own self-awareness by reflecting on Box 1.1:

Box 1.1: Teacher Self-Talk

Think about it: the "me" that I know has been developing for many years. My knowledge of myself at this point in time is a composite of what I've heard about myself, what I've thought and felt about myself, and how I've acted in the world up to now. Can I remember any moment in my life that was particularly important to building my own self-awareness? How did I experience that moment or period of time? What self-knowledge did it leave me with? What did I learn about myself?

Basic Definitions

At this point it may be helpful to clarify terms we use throughout the book, as we differentiate between emotions, feelings, emotional information, reflection, self-talk and self-awareness. These definitions may also be useful for discussion in a middle school science class on brain anatomy. Antonio Damasio (1999, p. 42) explains:

the term *feeling* should be reserved for the private, mental experience of an *emotion* while the term *emotion* should be used to designate the collection of responses, many of which are publicly observable. In practical terms this means you cannot observe a feeling in someone else although you can observe a feeling in yourself when, as a conscious being, you perceive your own emotional states. Likewise, no one can observe your own feelings, but some aspects of the emotions that give rise to your feelings will be patently observable to others.

In essence, emotions are biological and feelings are personal interpretation. Emotion (Griffiths, 1997) usually refers to universal emotions including happiness, sadness, fear, anger, surprise or disgust; and sometimes secondary emotions such as embarrassment, jealousy, guilt, pride. Thus, even for the experts the distinction between emotion and feeling often becomes difficult to recognize.

Self-talk is the silent dialogue within ourselves through which we consider, or *reflect* on our thoughts and feelings. *Emotional information* is what we refer to as the moment-to-moment "meaning making" of the experience of our feelings, emotions, physical body sensations and emotional memories. *Self-awareness* is the process of focusing on our thoughts and emotional information to understand where they come from and what they mean. It can be momentary, for example understanding a feeling in the moment, or the integration of impressions overtime, such as recognizing one's life purpose. Definitions of these and other terms important to our discussion are all covered in the glossary.

Using the Book to Bring Our Strategies to Your Classroom

As teachers and students become more self-aware of individual learning processes and classroom behavior patterns, they are better able to effectively manage their approach to classroom learning. This makes the classroom a less stressful place for both student and teacher, and promotes successful academics and a sense of well-being. What we have observed is that whatever the differences between students' learning processes, self-awareness can help each student recognize and take responsibility for learning. Additionally, because classroom learning takes place in a social context, self-awareness can broaden students' understanding and responsibility for actions and reactions to others in the classroom. Finally, the greater a teacher's awareness of self, the greater her capacity to comprehend individual learning differences of students without judgment.

Exhibit 1.4, at the end of this chapter, provides an overview of how *Understanding Emotions in the Classroom* can help teachers incorporate self-awareness, and particularly emotional awareness, into their differentiated teaching strategies. First, we explore the meaning of self-awareness in Chapters 1 and 2. In Chapters 3 and 4 we examine the different roles emotion plays in the learning processes of individual students. To help teachers adapt their teaching strategies to these different learning needs, we provide frameworks and skill-building competencies in Chapters 5, 7, 8 and 9. We also offer different methods for teaching these lessons: 1) making self-awareness *explicit* in existing lessons (Chapter 2); 2) introducing emotional learning technologies (Chapter 10); and 3) utilizing advertising materials that elicit emotional responses (Chapter 11).

Understanding Emotions in the Classroom provides perspective relevant to teachers at all grade levels. For example, Chapter 3 provides a simple framework for teachers to observe differences in their students in grades K-4. By grades 5-7, this same framework can be introduced to students to understand the influence of emotions for themselves. Chapters 4 and 5 introduce basic skills that can be implemented in elementary school, but are adaptable to middle school and high school as well. Chapter 6 summarizes how to incorporate emotional information effectively into classroom learning at all levels. Chapters 7-9 explore self-awareness lessons that are developmentally appropriate for middle and high school, while also giving elementary teachers perspective on readiness skills.

Chapters 12 and 13 take us full circle back to the role of a teacher's own self-awareness in modeling the behavior and competency of self-awareness for students. Chapters 14-15 help us to reflect on how to introduce these strategies in our classrooms and schools as a whole.

Moving Into Your Own Classroom

In Chapter 2, we provide a framework for considering how self-awareness is currently tacitly going on in your classroom. The SOURCE framework will help you identify opportunities that are already at your fingertips. But remember our rules for including reflection and self-awareness in your curriculum:

- Learning and teaching should be fun so don't consider anything you wouldn't enjoy doing with your students!
- You do not need to develop new curriculum. Use what you already do in ways that make self-awareness lessons explicit in your <u>existing</u> curriculum! And catch those teachable moments that arise everyday.

Exhibit 1.1

Developing Self-Awareness in Grades K-12

Grade Level Focus	Examples of Emerging Abilities
Grades K-5: **Emotional Awareness Blossoms**	1) Find and name their feelings 2) Identify that their own feelings have a range and intensity that may be different than others 3) Understand they can interpret feelings in different ways 4) Know how to separate awareness of feelings from action in response (impulse control)
Grades 6-8: **Identity Emerges** From Childhood to Adolescence	1) Comprehend the "idea of themselves"—their self concept 2) Understand patterns of emotional temperament 3) Aware of peer group dynamics
Grades 9-12: **Transition to Adult Life** From Adolescence to Adulthood	1) Understand "fit" to a certain work or occupation direction 2) Determine values, natural abilities and interests that may suggest a life purpose or pursuit

Exhibit 1.2

Self-Awareness Builders Versus Busters

Child says:	Awareness Buster	Awareness Builder
"I'm starving."	"You can't possibly be hungry—you just came back from lunch."	"Wow! You must be growing. We have a break in 30 minutes. Tell your stomach to be patient."
"I'm really worried about the math test."	"Don't be silly—I'm sure you did fine."	"I can understand that tests can be worrisome. But you usually do well, and we'll know the results in a couple of weeks."
"I don't feel like I belong in that group—I'd like to change groups."	"I know this is going to be the right group for you."	"I know you might be uncomfortable with some people you don't usually work with, please try it for two weeks, and then we'll talk again."
"I hate Adam—he's a dork."	"Come on now, you don't really mean that."	"Hate is a strong feeling. Did something happen between you and Adam?"
"I'm really happy I got a B+ in math."	"Just keep working and you'll get an A."	"Great! You worked really hard. I'm happy for you too."

Exhibit 1.3

Self Awareness: Different Levels of Meaning

Definition: Self Awareness	Example
Simple response to a question	How am I feeling? I am feeling angry.
Integration of thoughts, feelings and behavior into a larger picture	Why did I say something rude to my teacher? I guess I was still angry at the fight I had with my friend on the way to school, and took it out on my teacher.
Attention to feelings, moods and their accompanying physical sensations; and our becoming aware of their source	I have a stomachache because I feel stressed about an exam.
Perceptions, impressions and judgements we develop of ourselves through reflecting on our strengths and personal challenges	I know I'm good in math and science and I like those subjects. I can imagine being a scientist.
Perspective on self, values and life purpose	I have strong scientific skills and value contributing to my community. Perhaps my calling is to discover a cure for a life-threatening illness.

Exhibit 1.4:

Developing Differentiated Teaching Strategies to Build Self-Awareness

Major Goals	Specific Objectives	Chapter References
Understand and teach the explicit meaning of self awareness, with emphasis on emotional awareness	Define the role of the emotional brain in learning Define self-awareness Define emotional information	Chapter 1 Chapters 1 & 2 Chapter 6
Understand differences in the role emotion plays for different students while learning, and for different teachers while teaching	Understand differences in human ynamics Understand differences in intensity of feelings during learning	Chapter 3 Chapter 4
Be able to teach a range of skills and frameworks that enable students to understand emotional learning differences and develop targeted skills for competency building	Understand and teach social problem solving skills Understand and teach differences in patterns of stress Understand and teach innersense Understand and teach peer feedback	Chapter 5 Chapter 7 Chapter 8 Chapter 9
Be comfortable teaching these lessons through a range of different methods	Teach material explicitly in existing lesson Integrate digital technology Integrate advertising media	Chapter 2 Chapter 10 Chapter 11

2
Teachable Moments in Your Classroom

Self-awareness can be an important motivator and enhancer of student learning. The student who recognizes her way of learning as unique and powerful proudly enters the classroom arena. Unfortunately, many students see their unique ways of learning as weaknesses that need to be fixed. We help these students become self-aware of the strengths of their natural approach to learning, where they will learn most easily, and where they may have to work a bit harder. We can help them to understand how to motivate themselves to study and learn subjects that they may naturally find disinteresting or boring. Indeed, becoming self-aware about one's learning process is an important part of our strategies for differentiating the classroom as students move from grades K-12.

The SOURCE model is a useful tool for bringing self-awareness into the classroom in a practical way. The six letters of SOURCE represent six dimensions of self-awareness that can help students better understand their potential for learning while helping teachers build curriculum that promotes self-reflection and understanding. **SOURCE** stands for:

Self-Regulation
Outlook
Uniqueness
Resilience
Connection
Energy

The SOURCE framework (See exhibit 2.1, at the end of this chapter) helps teachers think through their existing curriculum to identify places that offer natural opportunities to enhance their lessons with self-awareness objectives. You are invited to take a closer look at these important elements and to add others or use your own as fits your classroom. Each of these elements points to an aspect of self that students are able to observe about themselves, at appropriate developmental stages, with the help of their teachers and parents. When students gain this self-awareness, they have the capacity to more effectively develop their full academic potential. They will begin to recognize how their personal qualities can contribute to the way they approach their academic learning.

In the next few pages, the SOURCE model will be explored in the following three ways:

- Defining the meaning of each element of the SOURCE model.
- Suggesting questions for teachers to use in exploring their own experiences with this dimension of classroom learning. (These questions are presented in boxes accompanying the definition.)
- Sharing ideas other teachers have developed for integrating each dimension of SOURCE into an existing lesson or class module.

Teachers are advised to focus on parts of their curriculum where they feel it would be enjoyable to try a fresh approach!

Box 2.1: Author Self-Reflection (Claudia)

In teaching self-awareness approaches to students and other teachers I have learned the value of using consistent words and definitions to describe "what we are becoming aware of." It is also important to give a name to what we want students to recognize and honor. For this reason I developed the SOURCE model, which I have shared with teachers around the country. Many of the behaviors described in this Chapter are things we do everyday in our classes. However, until they are assigned a definition, they often do not become a conscious part of our classroom experience. This has been particularly true in teaching students, where I find it is simply not enough to model appropriate behavior. I have been surprised to experience how important the link between self-awareness and shared, common vocabulary is in developing student recognition and skill-building. That is why I find the SOURCE framework so useful to teachers and students, who are studying self-awareness.

Self-Regulation

Self-regulation refers to the handling of our reactions to our feelings and impulses. As early as preschool, children can be taught to observe and modify their approaches to self-regulation. For example, 5-year-old Sarah's teacher can observe, "Sarah, I see you knocked the blocks down when you got angry with Julie. Let's use words to tell Julie you are angry. What words do you want to say to tell Julie to let her know that you are angry?"

Children and adults alike need to examine their strategies for self-regulation. They need to learn to calm down when upset and to steady themselves when overcome by strong emotions of any kind. For example, Jane, a seventh grader, demonstrates effective awareness of her ability to self-regulate as she identifies her feelings and related actions under stress. "When I am taking a timed test, I feel really stressed out," she says. "My hands get very icy and my brain gets blurry and my adrenaline gets going. I notice that if I get up to go to the bathroom and then come back and start to work on the test, my brain settles down and I can think straight and start solving the problems."

When teachers become aware of their own approaches to self-regulation, as illustrated in Box 2.2, they can more effectively teach this skill to students:

Box 2.2: Self-Talk Exercise #1

How do I feel when a student is disrespectful to me? What is it I do to manage my feelings in the situation? Is this method one that lets me understand and work with the feelings so they don't fester inside? If not, how can I find an alternative approach that will help me to manage my feelings in a way that helps me to feel better, work effectively and see my student more clearly?

There are many ways in which teachers can effectively teach students to be aware of alternative approaches to self-regulation. For younger children, reading a story about a child who is acting out in some way, such as fighting, provides an opportunity to analyze the underlying feeling the character is facing, and develop alternate ways the character can handle the situation. Another example for younger children is *Fun with Feelings*, an introductory class on emotional literacy for pre-schoolers, where children learn about their individual ways of self-regulating by focusing on one feeling at a time, i.e. anger, sadness, nervousness, and then sharing their individual strategies with their classmates.

A middle-school math teacher asks students to brainstorm their fears about math at the beginning of the semester. He then asks them to write down each of their anxieties on a piece of paper and put the paper in a box. Throughout the semester, the students practice calming themselves when they are unable to think clearly, and keep journals about the self-regulation techniques they use to reduce their anxiety. Once they feel they have mastered a particular anxiety, they remove its respective paper from the box. The ultimate goal is for each student to have an empty box by the end of the term, revealing that they are leaving the anxiety behind and have effectively mastered the appropriate self-regulation skills.

As a result of dealing directly with student math-anxiety, this math teacher found a significant amount of increased time for teaching math. Many teachers can find similar approaches to teaching effective self-regulation strategies in other classes.

Box 2.3: Self-Talk Exercise #2

Are there specific students in my class who need to develop awareness of self-regulation capabilities? Is there an activity where I could support my students in discussing the strategies they use for self-regulation, and where they can offer each other tips?

Outlook

Our outlook includes our attitudes and beliefs that influence how we approach the world. This is a self-awareness skill that students start to develop in their early years as they listen to their own self-talk, which includes statements such as:

- Everything will turn out okay!
- Nothing ever works out for me.
- My life is great.
- I can't do anything right; my brain never works.
- The world is safe.
- It doesn't matter how much I study; I just can't get it.
- Things just seem to work out for me; I always look on the positive side.
- The world will blow up before I am an adult.

Outlook has a significant impact on school performance. If students believe that the world is a hopeful place and that their actions can make a difference, there is a reason to study and work harder. If, on the other hand, they believe the world is not hopeful and that no matter what they do they are doomed to fail, why bother? In their modeling, stories, and responses, teachers can explain how positive or negative attitudes can influence performance.

Ninth grader Wyatt demonstrates an awareness of his outlook when he develops a picture of options for his life after high school: "I have an ability to take risks and chances without much apprehension. I am willing to jump right into a problematic situation and try whatever seems to work. I could see myself after college in a job where I would be dealing with risk in business. I would never make the same mistake twice. Yet scattered among the work, there would have to be some fun for me to be happy and satisfied with my life."

In contrast, eighth grader Matthew talked consistently about the futility of studying for any test. After the World Trade Center disaster in New York, he saw his teachers, and the world at large, as unpredictable. He believed that no matter how much he studied he may not do well, and that he had no control over his grades (or his life). By talking about his beliefs in class and committing to change his perspective, he was able to adopt a more positive outlook. He decided to just give his best effort. The consequences in grade outcome were positive for him.

Box 2.4: Self-Talk Exercise #3

What is my outlook on life? How does being aware of it give me an advantage? What is my outlook on my class this year? What is my outlook on being a teacher?

A fifth grade teacher in Connecticut includes a module on pioneers in his history curriculum. The class studies different groups who immigrated to the United States and others who crossed the country. Part of the module asks the students to become pioneers themselves, by converting the number of books they read on their own into miles crossed on the road to from Connecticut to California. The teacher introduces the idea of outlook by brainstorming the outlook of the pioneers at the outset of their journey. How did they maintain a positive attitude in the face of poor weather, hunger, and rough roads?

Next, the teacher turns to the question of his "classroom pioneers." What is the attitude or outlook the students have on reading? Do they have a sufficiently positive outlook to believe they can read enough books to "cross the country?" If their feelings are negative, how can they identify feelings and their consequences and choose alternate strategies to deal with their negative feelings? What positive feelings do they have about the journey, and how can they develop strategies to build on those positive feelings? In this way, children learn to modify their attitudes and change their outlook.

As the students take tests and attempt to accomplish other goals, the teacher often brings them back to discuss awareness of their outlook. When an individual or the group as a whole suffers feelings of defeat, the teacher has them practice identifying their feelings and examining their consequences to become aware of self-regulating approaches for re-gaining a positive outlook.

A seventh-grade math teacher examines the question of outlook in a different way. She explains that math gives us a way to understand the outlook of the class by tabulating statistics on information class members report. For example, in her class on mean, median, and mode, she has the class vote numerically on their values, assigning a rank order to a list of seven values: friendship, family closeness, personal attractiveness, integrity, athleticism, intelligence, adventure. She then computes the mean, median, and mode for the reported values, and explains to the class that these statistics are a way of representing the class' outlook on values. This leads to a discussion of how values contribute to the outlook of the class. The students pick up the discussion with their English teacher when they look at different periods in history and try to determine the values held by people during each period based on information from their readings.

An art teacher shares another very different perspective on out-look. In her high school art class she studies different forms of artistic expression, from traditional to modern. In viewing different artwork with her students, she asks them to comment on the outlook of the historical period in which the artwork was created to observe how the artist cap-tures the period. For example she comments, "One -point perspective represents a rather materialistic (and even imperialistic) outlook. The joyful color of Matisse presents a totally subjective outlook." The students can carry this impression of different outlooks into a discussion in their history class, where differences in attitudes and values of the period can provide another interesting perspective on one's outlook.

Box 2.5: Self Talk Exercise #4

Which of my students need to develop a more positive outlook? How can I help them to understand the feelings that may block a positive outlook? What is my outlook for today? For the year? For the semester?

Uniqueness

Self-awareness of our uniqueness covers a lot of ground. How do we learn? How are we similar to classmates? How are we different? What are our temperaments and personalities like? For the purposes of our discussion here, how do all these aspects of uniqueness influence learning in the classroom? And how do we help students become aware of what makes them special and distinct?

Awareness of uniqueness is important to young children and can be encouraged in concrete ways. For example, awareness of their unique learning styles can help children build confidence and know-how in learning. Uniqueness includes many dimensions of a person, including learning style, body image and physical characteristics, stress responses, beliefs, personal and family history, individual gifts and challenges, likes and dislikes and leadership skills.

Kids love to discover and discuss their individual personalities, temperaments, and differences. In Human Growth and Development class, we share our observations about our own temperaments, and the consequences of our style in the classroom. Julie, for example, is a flamboyant eighth grader who expresses pride in her bold temperament style: "Some people keep their feelings locked. I enjoy confrontation. Confronting someone helps me deal with my feelings. It is my way of solving a problem. Some people think everything out, I don't, I just mainly react. I do not hide my thoughts. If you did something wrong you are going to hear about it." She also recognizes that these behaviors can sometimes get her into trouble when she talks before thinking things out.

Michael, in contrast, is an 11-year-old boy who recognizes his own temperament as more timid and upbeat. He is quiet and sensitive and proud of his sensitivity to others, and he prides himself on being important to groups of children who are particularly in need of sensitivity and care. He recognizes that his needs may sometimes be overlooked in situations where he doesn't speak up for himself.

Box 2.6: Self-Talk Exercise #5

How am I unique? How do I learn best? How do I take in information? What is my personality style? How would I describe my temperament? How does this impact my way of teaching? How would this exercise of considering uniqueness be useful to students?

A third-grade teacher discusses uniqueness by reading different books that demonstrate conflicts between kids. "I don't call it a temperament. That would be too abstract for my kids. But I encourage the class to consider how different children in the book respond to conflict. Some walk away, others become bullies, and some try to talk through the problem. We can try to understand the feelings of the characters in the situation, the problems underlying their feelings, and their alternative courses of action."

A seventh-grade science team decided to use the concept of temperament to understand differences in the way two scientists used the scientific method to develop their theories of evolution. The class then identified a Myers Briggs temperament (a self-awareness model which will be discussed in Chapter 8) for each scientist, and discussed the different ways each scientist used the scientific method in developing his theory. The differences were marked. This really brought the science class to life. Of course, students hotly debated the temperament types of each scientist. This reinforced the point that classifications are difficult and complex.

A ninth-grade history teacher in New Mexico used the Myers Briggs framework to help her students analyze the personality and approach of the Conquistadors who came to New Mexico. In this way the students were able to consider military strategy and speculate about the inner workings of the different personalities.

An eleventh-grade English teacher used a similar Myers Briggs approach to help students examine their uniqueness by having them reflect on their special gifts, their areas of personal power, their likes and dislikes, and their social patterns. In helping the students to prepare their college essays, the teacher asked them to write about how these strengths contribute positively to their classmates, their families, and their future careers. This helped the students to really focus deeply on examining their uniqueness.

Box 2.7: Self-Talk Exercise #6

What dimension of uniqueness would I like students to understand about themselves as a result of taking my class? How does this dimension help them to perform more effectively in the classroom? Where is there a place in my curriculum to bring this dimension to life? What distinctions do I think might emerge that could provide material for classroom differentiation strategies? What makes me unique as a teacher?

Resilience

Resilience is the ability to recover from or adjust easily to misfortune or change. Building resilience requires awareness of whether one is stymied by or learns from obstacles and set-backs. Resilience is critical for dealing with the often uncertain and pressured lives kids lead today. They need to be able to recognize changes in their environment, engage their imaginations to deal with those changes, and tolerate feelings of incompetence, loss, or failure, while learning to master new situations. Resilience is a key factor in school performance, health, and well-being.

High expectations often create the need for strong resiliency skills. For example, Jake, a popular eighth-grade student, was asked to drop out of student government because his grades fell below a certain level. Aware of his tendency to give up when things don't come easily, he made an extra effort to study for the next report period in the hopes that he could resume student government later in the year.

Box 2.8: Self-Talk Exercise #7

How resilient am I? How do I handle students who have great difficulty in learning? Do I give up? Where do I find the strength to seek new ways of teaching? How do I handle the stresses of long workdays? What ways do I have of strengthening my own resilience that I can share with students?

A biology teacher designed his curriculum to include resilience in his discussion of the ecosystem. What animal species seemed especially resilient? Which seemed less resilient, thereby risking extinction? How does one part of the ecosystem affect the resiliency of other parts and of the system as a whole? This discussion easily transferred to a discussion on success and failure of students. How do some students bounce back from failure and become successful again?

A history teacher brought up the subject of resilience when looking at political figures such as Richard Nixon and Bill and Hillary Clinton. How did these people have enough resilience to keep reinventing themselves?

In both of these classes, the teachers helped students to identify feelings associated with defeat, learn how to understand these feelings and their consequences, and then redefine the problem to look for ways to increase resilience through self-regulation strategies. The process of sharing personal stories of overcoming obstacles also built strong bonds between the students, enhancing the safety of the learning environment.

An art teacher worked on resilience in relation to the development of ceramic-wheel skills. English teachers have many opportunities to discuss resilience in characters of books they read. Science teachers can talk about resilience in nature. The important lesson for students is to become aware of the feelings that keep them from responding proactively to set-backs, and develop ways to bounceback.

Connection

Awareness of connection is the understanding of how we relate to others in personal relationships, groups, and communities. Connection includes awareness of points of view other than our own. This perspective taking builds empathy. Connection also includes awareness of how we communicate, make friends, resolve conflicts, and collaborate as learners.

Initially, children learn many of their connecting skills by way of the attention they receive from parents at early ages, as well as by watching their parents interact. Later in life, peers, teachers, and other adults instill connecting skills by communicating and providing feedback to young children. For example, Jerry, a shy second grader, learned that he could get attention from other kids by making a scary face. By fifth grade, other kids were still reinforcing this habit of Jerry's through their comments: "Jerry! The teacher's not looking. Show us your scary face."

Teachers, too, gave Jerry the greatest attention when he was acting out. The attention may have been disciplinary, but it was still the most attention that Jerry received. By seventh grade, Jerry did not yet realize that the scary face was also making him the laughing stock of the class. He needed to become more aware of alternative ways to connect with other people.

Awareness of how and why we connect is important to becoming a part of the school community. We can help increase this awareness by understanding our unique personality styles. Connecting with teachers and other students is a critical way of exchanging ideas. Imagine how much more successful the conversations between teachers, students and peers can be when students are aware of the effectiveness of their connections.

Box 2.9: Self-Talk Exercise #8

How do I connect to students? Do I move close when they move close? Do I move away? Do I initiate contact? Do I wait to be asked? Is this different for me with individuals in contrast to groups? What is the character of my personal connection? For example, am I typically serious, sarcastic, warm or distant? In what way does this affect the impact of my teaching?

Foreign language teachers have the potential to build on connection awareness as they teach the words for meeting new people, starting up conversations, and managing discussions. As one drama teacher pointed out, "I have all sorts of exercises where I use true connection between people—real listening and being in the moment with the other actor or actors on stage. So many of the exercises reveal to the students where they are emotionally. Are they holding back? Are they throwing up a smokescreen so that the other performers are not let in? How do their expressions communicate the role they are playing?"

One fourth grade teacher used a life-issues lesson on making friends to help her students understand just how they approach others in the room, and to help them to be aware of which of these approaches works for them and which does not. For example, Isabella is aware that she always asks a question when she approaches another child, such as "How are you? What'cha been doing? Can I join you?" She thinks of this as being polite and believes it is a successful strategy. Sirra does it differently. She makes a statement that is a compliment to the other. Sirra might say, "Great to see you!" "You are the BEST FRIEND, I want to talk to you for just a minute." She also finds this to be a successful way to make connections. Lea is not so successful and has difficulty identifying her strategies for approaching others. She found it very helpful to listen to others and learn from their strategies.

Energy

Awareness of your level of energy, your presence, and your physical wellness also helps contribute to the learning process. We all know people who enter a room and "take up a lot of space," "command a lot of presence," or "attract a lot of attention." Others come in and "have a soothing way" or "make us feel safe." People communicate their well-being, stance, voice, and attitude nonverbally. Most children implicitly recognize these factors in peers and in the adults around them. Critical to this aspect of awareness is an understanding of how your energy affects others in the room; realistic self-appraisal is essential for fostering relationships.

Though he is only five feet tall, Richard has a strong physical presence. When standing in front of the class, the teacher's eye travels often toward him, probably because he is so energetic. Because of his strong physical presence, Richard's actions — including any misbehavior—command a lot of attention.

On the other hand, Alice seems quiet when approached. The teacher does not readily notice her when scanning the class. Alice's energy moves inward; she can do the same things as Richard and not be noticed. Alice recognizes her inner presence: "Sometimes I feel like no one sees me," she says. Yet Alice can be more effective than Richard during conflicts, helping people to relax and settle down. She manifests calm and quiet, and people are influenced by her non-intrusive presence. Unfortunately, since teachers more quickly notice Richard than Alice, he receives more attention than she does. As a result, Alice may grow to see her quiet energy as only a weakness rather than a source of strength, unless others help her to understand where her real strength lies.

Box 2.10: Self-Talk Exercise #9

What do I know about my presence in a room? How would I describe my energy level? Does it impact my teaching? Are there some of my students who seem to get a lot of attention because they are high energy? Do some students get overlooked because their energy is quiet?

The drama teacher works with energy in terms of stage presence: Does the actor's energy move toward the audience? Is it centered? Is the actor's energy pulling away and drawing the other actors toward him or the audience? Students study the nonverbal techniques that help move an individual's energy in one way or another. One dean of freshman studies talked about a high school orientation exercise in which students explore their physical presence through role-playing: the students are asked to imagine themselves in another person's shoes and walk around the room trying on different learning and communication styles.

Practicing Self-Awareness

The most effective way for both teachers and students to develop their skills in self--awareness is to regularly take a step back and consider their own thoughts and feelings. In the fast-paced and demanding contemporary school environment, we can easily become focused on asking questions about everything but our own inner workings. SOURCE is a comfortable, inclusive guide for focusing on our own inner processes. It is a reflective guide that can bring new information to our classrooms to create more effective learning processes for both teachers and students.

In this chapter, we have set aside reflection boxes, which ask you to reflect on your own thoughts and feelings about the material being covered. Throughout the rest of the book, we will share with you various teacher self-reflections, as well as our own self-reflections. To emphasize these thoughts and feelings, we have set them apart in boxes. You may find that taking the time to read the box interrupts your reading. That is our intention: we want you, and your students, to learn to take a moment to check in with yourself and shift your focus briefly, so that you can process your thoughts and feelings and refresh yourself. We encourage you to cultivate this habit in the classroom, for both yourself and your students. It is the core skill for effectively building self-awareness.

Box 2.11: Author Self-Reflection (Robin)

I have learned that the process of self-awareness is critical to my own growth as an educator and psychotherapist. Over the years I have seen the need to devote more and more time to it—stopping the "noise" all around me, and taking a moment or two to reflect on my feelings, thoughts and actions. I find that when I take that time to think about how I am connecting to people, how I am learning, what is in the way of my being more effective in the workplace, I can think more clearly and strategize more effectively. I know that helping young people reflect on how they learn, how they communicate, and how they approach the world will make it possible for them to make positive choices and strategize for more success in the classroom and with their friends.

Exhibit 2.1

SOURCE® Dimensions of Self-Awareness

SELF-Regulation: Awareness of feelings and impulses, and making decisions about how to deal with them

OUTLOOK: Perspective on oneself or one's life

UNIQUENESS: Awareness of what makes a person special and distinct

RESILIENCE: Awareness of adaptability to recover from misfortune and change

CONNECTION: Awareness of one's process of relating to others as partners, groups and communities

ENERGY: Awareness of the impact of physical presence

® Claudia Marshall Shelton, 1997

3

Differentiating the Experience of Emotion

Does the experience of emotion while learning play different roles in different children? That is a complex question. In Chapter 3, we introduce an approach that can help teachers, students and parents to identify students for whom emotion plays a particularly important role in the learning process, in contrast to those for whom emotion may play a less significant role. Some students, for instance, will plunge enthusiastically into class discussions and say the first thing that comes to mind, while others will hold back, think carefully about what they say and express little or no emotion. Students handle stress differently, too: while some seem to thrive on grade competition, others get so tense that their work performance suffers. There are children who prefer to work by themselves, and ones who will wither unless they can talk to their friends.

Human Dynamics and Social-Emotional Differentiation

In order to deal with emotional differences among students using classroom differentiation strategies, I developed a contract-setting approach that uses the Human Dynamics model to help teachers and students understand their social-emotional preferences for learning. Developed in 1979 by Sandra Seagal and her colleagues, the Human Dynamics work has involved over 40,000 people from more than 25 cultures, and is being used currently by teachers in over 11 countries throughout the world. Human Dynamics identifies inherent distinctions in the ways people communicate, relate to others, solve problems, stress out. Seagal refers to these distinctions as "dynamics," and identifies them as "mentally-centered, " "emotionally-centered, " and "physically-centered" (See Exhibit 3.1 at the end of this chapter), without regard to race, age, culture, or gender.

Every individual encompasses elements of all three dynamics (See Exhibit 3.2 at the end of this chapter); however, one of the three dynamics will most likely be dominant, a second will be subordinate, and the third, tertiary. In working with children I refer only to the dominant dynamic.

> **Box 3.1: Author Self-Reflection (Claudia)**
>
> I have used the Human Dynamics Model with students, parents and other teachers many times over the past seven years, and have learned to watch for a cultural preference that often arises in our study. Sandra Seagal told me that she sees the "emotionally-centered" learner as the most prevalent dynamic in the United States. My experience reinforces this, and it can set a certain judgmentalism in motion: When some parents or teachers in the United States observe the Human Dynamics video (see Step 1 below) of different students, they express a subtle positive bias toward the "emotionally-centered child" and a critical attitude toward the other dynamics. Recognizing the bias being expressed is very important in helping these individuals appreciate the value in all dynamics. Once parents and teachers become aware of potential bias, they are usually careful to keep their discussion "dynamic-neutral." I have not yet experienced this judgment in children when they view the video. I work hard to keep it from cropping up in my own attitude.

Although I use the Human Dynamics model with students in late elementary school, teachers and parents may also use it to understand learning differences among younger students. My approach includes a four-step process that helps students realize how their social-emotional abilities affect their learning.

- **Step 1.** Students at the fifth or sixth grade level study the Human Dynamics framework in order to reflect on their learning processes, paying particular attention to the roles of emotion, temperament, and social-emotional skills. I introduce this by having the students view a video called "Park Design" (Human Dynamics Video, www.humandynamics.com, 1999).
- **Step 2.** The teacher and students discuss the learning dynamics as identified by each student.
- **Step 3.** With the perspective on their personal choice of best-fit dynamic, the students complete a contract that specifies any social and emotional skills they would like to strengthen.
- **Step 4.** Each student meets monthly with the teacher to discuss progress on goals, focusing on student awareness and self-reflection rather than on teacher evaluation. Students sometimes change the objectives for their social and emotional skills objectives in these discussions.

Human Dynamics in Action

Let's join Mr. Christopher's fifth grade class as they follow the four-step model. He begins by introducing Human Dynamics to his class through a viewing of the "Park Design" video. Mr. Christopher is very concerned about the emotional tone he sets in introducing the framework, as reflected in Box 3.2.

Box 3.2: Mr. Christopher's Self-Reflection

I intend to provide students with a framework for developing their self-reflective skills, and to help them become aware of how they naturally learn so that they can take responsibility for that process. It is not important for them to categorize themselves. There is no right or wrong answer. This is no place for judgmental thinking; I hope I can effectively communicate this to the class.

Mr. Christopher specifically wants his students to identify for themselves the role that emotion, temperament, and social-emotional skills play in the learning process. Viewing a video will help them to observe these differences on their own. The "Park Design" video shows three-minute clips of groups of fifth graders representing the different dynamics. Each group is assigned the task of creating a tabletop model of a park. Though each group is given identical instructions and materials to create their ideal park, each goes about the task in very different ways. Implicit in each group's performance are differences in learning dynamic and emotional temperament.

Understanding Emotionally-Centered Learners

After watching the video, Mr. Christopher's class discusses the different groups. While several students don't think they fit into any of the groups in terms of their learning dynamics, about half see themselves as "emotionally-centered learners." As one student notes: "This group is having the most fun! They never stop talking, and enjoy being together."

Emotionally-centered students like to connect with one another personally as they work. They appear emotionally expressive and enjoy working spontaneously and interacting socially. These learners prefer a classroom-learning situation that provides:

- An environment of mutual support and respect;
- Lessons and presentations that have color and imagination;
- Opportunities to express their creativity and dramatization;
- Frequent opportunities to move around, talk, and work collaboratively in groups;

This group of learners has a strong interest in emotion and feelings, their own and those of others. They are interested in subjects about people, and are often naturally adept at skills related to social interaction.

Understanding Mentally-Centered Learners

Only one of Mr. Christopher's students identifies himself as "mentally-centered." This student says the characteristic that he identifies with most is "the desire to work quietly alone."

The three mentally-centered children in the video choose to work independently. Each builds his own separate park in contrast to the single, shared park development chosen by the emotionally-centered group. The mentally-centered learners work with careful attention to detail, do not talk, and respect one another's spaces. The parks that result are symmetrical and orderly, and two of the three parks that result do not include exhibits of people.

In terms of the social-emotional abilities they demonstrate, these children show a natural preference for working alone and less of an interest in engaging socially. This does not mean that these children cannot be skillful in managing social situations. Instead, they have a natural temperament toward working independently. They may find too much social interaction to be tiring.

Mentally-centered learners prefer learning situations that provide:

• An initial overview of any topics to be presented;
• A clear statement of the value and purpose of any lesson;
• A learning process that is structured and logical;
• Opportunities to work and read alone.

This group of learners naturally express a skill-set which others might label "self-regulation." The mentally-centered learner would see this not as a skill, but as a way of being in the world.

Understanding Physically-Centered Learners

About one-third of Mr. Christopher's students identify with the physically-centered learners. One of these girls notes in viewing the video, "Their park looks like a real park, and it offers rides that work. They even have signs to show how much it costs to go on a ride. We're interested in things that really work."

In the video, we see a group of children who appear practical and focused in their approach to the task. They work together to build a joint park, which is realistic and similar to an actual park in their geographic vicinity. Their conversation is about the task at hand. Their final product is substantial and detailed, and it features workable structures.

The natural social-emotional abilities these children demonstrate are related to the awareness of the group as a unit. Their conversation clarifies the relationship between themselves and other members of the group in completing their task. They organize their work with the group's ideas and capabilities in mind. While the members of emotionally-centered group relate personally, the members of the physically-centered group relate operationally. They determine what they are going to produce together, and each focuses on building his or her part. While they sometimes communicate in words, much of their communication is nonverbal. Each student appears aware of what the others are doing and shapes his or her contribution accordingly.

The physically-centered learner prefers learning situations that provide:

- A clear understanding of the practicality of any lesson;
- Abstract concepts that are illustrated with concrete examples;
- When possible, sensory, tactile experience for what is being taught;
- Context and content of the material clearly defined to illustrate the interconnections among the parts of the whole;
- Sufficient time to absorb and integrate new material, to complete tasks, and to consider questions before responding.

These children may be interested in feelings, but have a natural focus on awareness of group dynamics in accomplishing a task.

Writing Papers for Self-Awareness

Mr. Christopher tells the class, "Our goal is not to type ourselves but to use the video, and the words we use to describe it, as a way of learning important information about ourselves." He then asks the students to complete a short paper describing their approach to learning and the social-emotional skills they feel they rely on most and least. The students are told that they can approach the assignment using the information presented in the video to help describe themselves. As an alternative, they can develop their own model to describe themselves, although that is probably more difficult.

It is vital for each student to self-reflect and describe the role of emotion and social--emotional skills in their learning process. They will next develop a contract with Mr. Christopher to identify those social-emotional skills that they want to develop over the coming term. The students' papers demonstrate a range of understanding to Mr. Christopher, and he thinks a lot about the exercise before meeting individually with students to discuss their contracts.

Box 3.3: Mr. Christopher's Self-Reflection

Self-reflection is a difficult process to learn to do well. I was not as interested in the results of the written work as I was in the thinking process that the students went through to see themselves. I want to use the contract-setting as a way to build student confidence and to help them understand the influence of social and emotional skills on their learning, from their own personal perspective. In setting their contracts, I want each student to think through skill-building in the social-emotional arena that they believe would help them to learn—whether this is awareness of others in a group setting, being aware of feelings and learning self-regulation techniques that help with classroom attention, practicing being a more active participant in group discussions, or a range of other skills. I want them to recognize that we can build social and emotional skills in the same way we build math or reading skills: by focus, discipline and practice.

Setting Contracts

The student's contract is the written agreement that results from the student-teacher discussion about the specific social-emotional skills the student would like to build, with specific identification of a plan. Let's see what each of three students discusses with Mr. Christopher, and the goals they set in their contract.

Amanda, the Emotionally-Centered Learner

In her paper, Amanda identifies herself as an emotionally-centered learner, but with some of the characteristics of a physically-centered learner. She describes herself as someone who learns by communicating with others. The teacher's opinion of her is very important to Amanda. She also feels a strong need to use her creative imagination.

When Mr. Christopher asks Amanda about her need to talk often with friends in class, she says, "It's just I get bored doing the same thing for too long. Each class point makes me think of something I need to share with Sandy."

Mr. Christopher tells her that her talking is often distracting to him and interrupts the class. She is surprised that he notices what she is doing, and agrees to try talking with Sandy only during the break. Mr. Christopher says he will give a short stretch break in the middle of class so that any students who need to move around will have a way to reduce their restlessness. Amanda is pleased with this idea.

From her self-defined perspective, Amanda can view her behavior not as something wrong but as a natural function of her personality. Yet she can also recognize that she needs to self-manage her behavior to meet classroom needs. In her contract, Amanda identifies a desire to work on a project assignment with someone whose way of learning is not relational in its orientation, most likely a mentally-centered or physically-centered learner. In this way, she thinks she can observe and discuss additional methods of self-regulation. Amanda also agrees to develop a class presentation on how to incorporate greater self-regulation skills into her way of doing things. These skills would include saving her comments for an appropriate occasion, writing notes to herself to remember what she wants to tell her friends after class, and stress--reduction exercises. Amanda is quite excited about beginning her project.

Roberto, the Mentally-Centered Learner

Roberto describes himself as closest to the mentally-centered students in the video. He recognizes that he likes to work alone, has a high need for privacy, and is organized and structured in his approach to learning. When Mr. Christopher asks why he seems to sit and stare into space in class, Roberto clarifies that he is not inattentive but simply does not need interaction to learn effectively. He further notes that his lessons are always in on time, his plan book is organized, and his academic performance is always high. He does not believe that his lack of interest in social chatter is a weakness; in fact, he notes that some others in the class can be distracting in their need to talk a lot.

As they talk further, Mr. Christopher discusses with Roberto how his desire to work alone might limit his flexibility in group-project work, which will increase in coming grades. In groups, Roberto may be working with others who have a higher need for feedback and interaction than he does. This seems logical to Roberto, who agrees that developing his skills for eliciting feedback might be an appropriate contract goal.

In the contract, Roberto notes his desire to work with a group of emotionally-centered learners who have a high need for interaction. As a result of this contract-setting process, Roberto has specific goals in mind for developing his social interaction skills. He also has a greater understanding of his teacher's need for classroom feedback from him—a step in the direction of empathy.

Andre, the Physically-Centered Learner

Andre tends to learn most effectively through sensory experience. He recognizes that he is practical and "hands-on" in his orientation, and describes himself as very aware of the social environment of the classroom. In fact, he claims to be so in touch with everything going on in class that he often doesn't know what to talk about first: "I get impressions about everybody and everything we are doing. Sometimes I just get information overload and don't know where to begin, so I just tune out."

Andre describes how he passes notes in class just to have something to do with his hands. He says he needs more physical activity to keep himself focused on the lesson; his mind absorbs too many facts, and he needs to walk around to feel grounded again. Unfortunately, as the classes get more abstract and discussion-oriented in sixth grade, he may have less opportunity for physical engagement than he did in the lower grades.

Andre thinks that his greatest social-emotional skill is in the area of awareness of himself and others around him: "I know what is happening to me and others around me. I just sometimes can't get the words fast enough to describe it. I may look fidgety, but don't think that I am not thinking about what is happening."

Andre decides to focus his contract on building self-management skills, particularly by using his laptop and sketching pad to try to more effectively capture his impressions of the class so that he can share them in an orderly way. In this way, he can either draw pictures or write paragraphs about what is happening. He also agrees to work on a project with Amanda, who is delighted by the prospect of having someone to appreciate her lively social skills. Mr. Christopher also tells Andre about the plan for a stretch -break in the middle of class so that students like him can integrate their thoughts as well as move around.

Reviewing the Exercise

Following the contract-setting discussions, the students became more absorbed in class and more attentive to managing their own social-emotional behavior in the classroom. This may have been a result of knowing that the little things they did were being noticed. By reflecting on their own inner processes within the contract-setting framework, the students have an easier time identifying opportunities for skill improvements. The role of the teacher as a "witness" to their process made the students feel appreciated and understood, rather than reflexively judged. Mr. Christopher was extremely pleased with the entire contract-setting approach, as related in Box 3.4

Energizing the History Class

Mr. Christopher was so excited about the self-reflective abilities that his students had demonstrated that he convinced Mrs. MacDonough, the history teacher, to try the approach in her lessons on Thomas Jefferson and Andrew Jackson. The students reflected on the facts they had learned about these two leaders and debated their learning dynamics.

Mrs. McDonough reported that the classroom felt electric during the debate on the different dynamics of these leaders. The students were highly motivated because, while learning about historical exhibits, they were at the same time engaging on a voyage of discovery about themselves and one another, reinforcing their commitment to understanding many significant dimensions of human differences.

Mrs. McDonough decided to build upon the students' enthusiasm by giving them an opportunity to strengthen their self-reflective abilities. She asked them to write a report on a historical figure they thought best represented their own personality dynamics. The list they could choose from included:
- Mental-Physical: Woodrow Wilson
- Emotional-Mental: Martin Luther King
- Emotional-Physical: Mother Teresa
- Physical-Emotional: Winston Churchill
- Physical-Mental: Nelson Mandela

Mrs. McDonough reported that the students were intrigued by this paper and worked hard to find data to support their thinking. Interestingly, those students who had previously had trouble conceptualizing ideas subsequently had no difficulty using the Human Dynamics framework to gather information and express their results. Like Mr. Christopher, Mrs. McDonough was amazed by her students ' capacity for reflection.

Exhibit 3.1

Defining The 3 Dynamics: Mental, Emotional, Physical

Mental

Thinking
Objectivity
Vision
Overview
Structure
Values

Emotional

Feeling
Subjectivity
Relationship
Communication
Organization
Creative Imagination

Physical

Doing
Making
Actualizing
Sensory Experience
Systemic Experience
Practicality

Exhibit 3.2

Learning With The 3 Dynamics

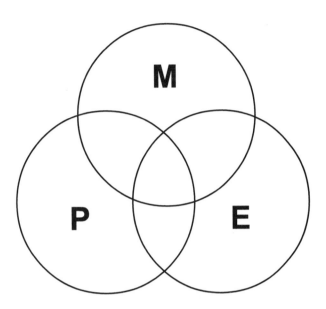

All people have the three dynamics, but one of the three is usually most dominant in their learning process.

4
Differentiating Intensity of Feelings

In this chapter we discuss the Resolving Conflict Creatively Program (RCCP), a school-based K-12 conflict resolution program created in 1985 by Linda Lantieri and Tom Roderick, through a joint initiative between the New York City Board of Education and the New York Chapter of Educators for Social Responsibility (Lantieri & Patti, 1996, p. 29). It is one of the largest programs of its kind, serving 400 schools and 175,000 students throughout the country. As you will soon see, a basic RCCP self awareness activity can help teachers develop strategies to differentiate the classroom using student understanding of the intensity of his or her emotional responses. Imagine how useful it is for teachers to know from the outset of the year, which children identify seemingly small slights as huge emotional wounds or which children are more likely than others to be really angry if recess is cancelled.

When students can understand their emotional intensity and related personal triggers, they are better able to partner with teachers in communicating this information. Consider Catherine, who is a very quiet, cooperative student until someone interrupts her when she is reading or working. Although many others in the class would be mildly annoyed by a similar disruption, Catherine turns beet red and starts yelling or crying. We can call her TOO sensitive and direct her to change her reaction. Or, we can be less evaluative and accept that this is the way this young girl responds, yet contemplate ways to enable her to develop strategies for more effective behavior. It is valuable information for Catherine's teacher to know that this student is not likely to be "ready" to learn during one of these emotionally intense times. The teacher might then develop a number of strategies:

- She can help Catherine learn more about her intense personal response, and find out if she likes it. Indeed, Catherine may be struggling to manage herself and in need of tools.
- If Catherine is willing to learn, the teacher can demonstrate calming techniques, such as deep breathing and counting.

(These skills will be presented in Chapter 5.) She can also be encouraged to write about her strong feelings as a means of self-regulation.

• The teacher can help Catherine choose a quiet workspace in the classroom to insure fewer interruptions that could trigger her intense reactions.

• Catherine can also prepare a list of phrases to alert people about how she feels about being interrupted, as well as choose work partners who are sensitive to similar issues. In this way, she learns to not allow her intense emotional reaction to get in the way of her connectivity to others in the class.

Visiting the Lab School

Let's visit a first grade class at the Lab School in New York City, an RCCP school where we will experience how emotional awareness is being taught to first graders in a way that helps them understand their varying intensities of emotional response to the same event.

Box 4.1: Author Reflection (Robin)

I chose the Lab School and this particular exercise —The Anger Thermometer— because I believe it illustrates very powerfully the link between self-awareness and the different learning needs of individuals within the classroom. It is the "surprise in the crackerjacks" in that, although the exercise is about self-awareness, it becomes immediately obvious that it is a segue to teaching diversity of reactions, tolerance for different viewpoints, and perspective taking. I participated in the exercise before including it in the book, and was fascinated by the responses of many students as they discovered for the first time that their own personal reactions were not necessarily shared by their friends. Also, many discovered that two people can experience a similar feeling such as anger with very different degrees of intensity. I highly recommend doing this exercise with your students!

First grade teacher Marjorie Martinelli considers the RCCP conflict resolution program to be extremely valuable for her students. Through this program, students become aware of themselves and their feelings, learn to appreciate the feelings and differences of others and build empathy. Today's lesson will first focus on learning that feelings are experienced at different levels of intensity by different people. The second goal is "perspective taking," understanding that not everything affects every person in the same way. People can react differently to the same event due to differences in personality, sensitivity, and experience. For example, if someone "smushes" Tamar's snack at snack time she would be angry;

Rebecca, however, would be furious, because she rarely gets to have a snack in the first place.

RCCP representative and facilitator, Jim Tobin, is present in class today, leading a warm-up activity called "Touch Blue," which is designed to increase students' awareness. He asks everyone to stand up. As the children look around the room, Jim says "Touch [an object or an adjective]," and the children have to look, find that something, and touch the person who is holding it. No hitting is allowed. One of the students asks if he can "pass," and a new rule is made: you can pass, but if you do, you'll have to actively watch. You cannot just sit in the back of the room, isolated from all the action.

Jim continues, asking students to touch a variety of things: leather (like shoes and belts), red, yellow, soft, curly, striped, brown, bumpy, hard. The children look around, yelling in excitement when they spot the desired object. The game gives everyone an opportunity to move around, interact with others, and, most importantly, become aware of their surroundings. The awareness developed here is an important precursor to the next activity, which will ask students to be aware of their inner experience.

After the children sit down and give themselves a big hand, Ms. Martinelli takes over the class and introduces The Anger Thermometer. The picture of the thermometer (See exhibit 4.1, at the end of this chapter) has markers for emotional intensity from mildly warm for annoyance to burning hot for rage, with increments of irritated, angry, and furious in between.

Ms. Martinelli encourages the students to shift their attention from "outside" to "inside" themselves. "Certain things make us angry," she says, "and there are different kinds of *angry*." She then elaborates on the different intensities of anger:

- "When today's assembly went on longer than it should have and took over our time, I was **annoyed**."
- "I get **irritated** when people ask me the same question over and over again."
- "I get **angry** if someone pushes me."
- "I get **furious** if they push me again."
- "I get **enraged** when I see children getting hurt."

Practicing with The Anger Thermometer in the Classroom

Now it is time for the students to practice using The Anger Thermometer (see Exhibit 4.1, at the end of this chapter) for themselves. Ms. Martinelli instructs them to pick a partner and fill out a handout, which describes four situations placed underneath a picture of thermometers. The four situations pictured are:

- Someone smushes your snack at snack time.
- A boy on the bus yells, 'You can't sit here! I own this seat!"
- A girl in the hall says, "You're a little kid and you should go to kindergarten."
- You want to use the swing, but the children who are on the swings won't get off.

The children identify how high up the anger scale each situation would take them and then compare their different reactions. Students are asked to come up with their own examples of situations that would make them feel enraged, furious, angry, irritated and annoyed. Before they actually begin the task, Ms. Martinelli asks them to repeat back the instructions. After finishing the assignment, the students are asked to share their comments about what the thermometer teaches them:

- "You can measure your feelings."
- "When you get more angry, you get more hotter."
- "I'm drawing on the outside what I'm feeling on the inside."

In order to "move down" the anger thermometer, most students choose such tactics as walking away, taking a break, and talking it out. As the children finish sharing their comments, the class ends. Ms. Martinelli has a few moments to reflect before moving to her next class:

Box 4.2: Ms. Martinelli's Self-Reflection

This was a really interesting class. I was filled with pride and joy watching my students come up with their own definitions of words. I was also relieved that my own expectations were not disappointed when the children had different responses to the same situation; they recognized this as the beginning of perspective taking. I noticed that I was thinking clearly and moving in sequence even though I did feel under pressure because we had a shortened period. I also liked the fact that this lesson lead nicely into perspective taking.

The students in Ms. Martinelli's classroom learn to identify how their emotional states influence problem solving. On one occasion, for example, the students are asked to name things they would like to change about the classroom. They report that what they feel strongest about is assigned seating, which is Ms. Martinelli's way of getting all the students to work with everyone else in the classroom, thus avoiding cliques and isolation. The students understand the reason behind Ms. Martinelli's seating arrangements, but they still want the opportunity to sit with friends and want permission to choose their own seats. Yet, being respectful of Ms. Martinelli's rationale and with their own feelings as a guide, they brainstorm a way that meets both their own and Ms. Martinelli's needs: choosing desk-partners each week, with the rule that they cannot sit with the same person all the time. Ms. Martinelli agrees to this. No slamming books. No tantrums. No sulking. Together they reach a win-win solution.

Ms. Martinelli is a Self-Aware Teacher, and uses this awareness to guide her decision making in the classroom. When she became aware of intense student feelings about controlling the class with her seating chart, she stepped back to reflect on the intensity of her own emotion. That momentary pause increased the likelihood that her choices would be driven by careful consideration of the issues at hand rather than the intensity of her feeling. Ms. Martinelli's simple reflection speaks to the heart of the RCCP philosophy—that we learn to work together in a collaborative way that respects our differences and reinforces our ability to mediate our conflicts constructively.

Focusing on Diversity

RCCP develops a school environment that values diversity and fosters cultural pride. This type of training is exactly what is needed to also understand that there is great diversity in how students respond to their emotional life and to events in the classroom that trigger emotional responses. Increasing an understanding of emotional differences between people is not dissimilar to the process of reducing prejudices between cultural groups: Students need to become aware of their emotional feelings, and learn to develop a vocabulary for discussing these feelings and prejudices. As this type of training must occur frequently in order to be effective, RCCP isn't meant to be just another lesson in the school day, but rather a philosophical shift in the way a school is organized and maintained.

Seeking Conflict Resolution and Avoiding Violence

RCCP recognizes the need for cooperative learning strategies in which group goals are established and students are individually held accountable for their work. The goal of RCCP is to create "peaceable" schools for children by ensuring that "young people develop the social and emotional skills needed to reduce violence and prejudice, form caring relationships, and create caring communities for learning" (Lantieri, 1997a, p. 157). Conflict resolution lies at the heart of the peaceable classroom and is supported by the synergy of five other principles:

cooperation, caring communication, appreciation of diversity, appropriate expression of feelings, and responsible decision making (Lantieri, L., and Patti, J., 1996a, p.27). When the curriculum reinforces these five themes, conflict resolution becomes possible. Fundamental to all of these principles is a need for students to become aware of thoughts and feelings that lock them into anger, prejudice, and potentially violent behavior. The goal is a change in attitude and a desire to teach students that they can generate alternative responses to violence.

Emotions Are The Driving Force of Learning

Teachers tell us there's a transformation that takes place for them when they embrace this work. They see alternate ways to manage their own responses. With practice of the skills they learn, and a deeper wisdom derived from self-reflection, they come to have more positive interactions with the people they care about in both their private and work worlds (1996a, pp. 122-123). The philosophy is translated to students in four ways (Lantieri & Patti, 1996, pp. 126-129a):

- "Direct teaching," in which teachers use prescribed lessons and units.
- "Teachable moments," in which teachers use community events and classroom occurrences to bring lessons into focus.
- Infusion of concepts into curriculum, such as language arts and math.
- Modeling, in which the teacher "walks the talk."

As Jim Tobin says, "Emotions are the driving force of learning." For active learning to take place, the classroom must not only be rich in emotional literacy but also filled with excitement. This occurs when children "feel" they are learning in an environment that addresses their individuality, interests, and educational and emotional needs—a safe and exciting environment for learning, where they feel both physically and emotionally secure, where they are able to recognize their feelings and express themselves without being judged.

Exhibit 4.1

Anger Thermometer

Name: _____

Someone smushes your snack at snack time.

A boy on the bus says, "You can't sit here. I own this seat."

A girl in the hall says, "You little kids should go to kindergarten."

You want to swing, but the children who are on the swings won't get off.

5
Building Basic Skills

Students' understanding of their own emotional patterns and skills can increase motivation and classroom attention. Students can develop contracts with their teachers, which identify skills that are well-developed and skills they need to strengthen. Teachers can then regularly provide students with feedback on their progress. Chapter 5 introduces some of these basic emotional skills, which students can develop in elementary grades.

At New Jersey's Bartle School social-emotional skills are actively being taught in grades K-5 using the *Social Problem Solving/Decision Making Model*, developed by Maurice Elias, John Clabby and Linda Bruene-Butler (see Elias, K.J. & Bruene-Butler, L., 1999). All teachers are trained to use the skills for classroom management, as lessons in their curricula, and to become more aware of their own feelings and stresses. As you read about Bartle, be aware of the composure of teachers and the overall positive school climate.

Box# 5.1: Author Reflection (Claudia)

I chose to visit Bartle because I believe it is a self-aware school: basic emotional awareness skills taught in the health curriculum are integrated into every subject, starting in kindergarten and developing progressively through fifth grade for all students—gifted, mainstream and special education. I had been trained in teaching the *Social Decision-Making Model* myself and respected its research-validated effectiveness. I made several visits to the school to observe K-5 classes in progress, taking particular note of how the basic skills were taught and practiced. In this chapter, I hope to let the reader view this impressive program as I experienced it.

Sharing a Common Language

Guidance Counselor Vicky Poedubicky recognizes the reason for the success of Bartle's emotional learning program:

> Being aware of and constructively managing emotions requires that both teachers and students share a common language and decision-making framework for learning. Yet what makes the skills become an integral part of academic learning is the work our teachers do in learning the skills themselves, modeling them for students, and actively building them into their day-to-day lesson plans.

In health classes from kindergarten through fifth grade, Bartle students practice social-emotional language and skills, and teachers integrate these skills into the discipline approach and guidance counseling process. The school's success is built upon emotional awareness on the part of both teachers and students.

"The reason the Bartle School program has been so successful over the 12 years I have been involved with it," says Linda Bruene-Butler, "is its commitment to professional development and *overlearning*. Research certainly shows that overlearning is fundamental to the teaching of skills based in emotional awareness." (Elias, M. J. and Bruene-Butler, L., 1999)

In terms of self-awareness, overlearning means being able to turn your attention to yourself time and time again, and practice the skill repetitively until it becomes automatic. For teachers and students to access emotional and social skills whenever they're under stress, they need to practice the skills until they become almost instinctive. Bartle's program fosters this repetitiveness via systemwide integration, making overlearning fundamental to the learning process.

Supporting Teachers with Professional Development

Professional development is essential for teachers to build and sustain their awareness levels. Consequently, all new teachers receive a five-week training program made up of weekly two-hour after-school sessions that helps them confidently integrate emotional learning into their classroom management and curriculum.

The importance of this professional development cannot be over-emphasized. This is where teachers learn the history, vocabulary, and classroom management techniques for building emotional awareness. This increased awareness of themselves and one another helps teachers become more emotionally present in the classroom, better able to model emotionally aware practices to students, and more supportive of one another in facing teaching challenges.

Working with Special Education Students

As we will demonstrate throughout the book, teachers can take the lead in creating a self-aware classroom. At the Bartle School, special education teachers recognized that as their students worked on social-emotional skills, they developed a broader range of decision-making tools. This enabled them to confidently leave their isolated special education learning classroom and move to a more inclusive class with general education students for some subjects each day.

"Raising the Bar"

Mrs. Lerner is a special education teacher. She teaches seven special needs students reading, spelling and math in one room, separate from the mainstream students in the adjoining classroom. Mrs. Lerner says she introduced emotional learning to special education students as a way to "raise the bar for these students to be like their peers, find talent in themselves, and use words not your hands to solve problems." For this class, called "Reading through Learning," the special needs children will join the mainstream students. We'll have the opportunity to observe Mrs. Lerner's class and also share her personal self-reflection.

Today Mrs. Lerner's mixed class is going to read "Angel Child, Dragon Child" by Michele Maria Surat. Before reading the book to the class, Mrs. Lerner reflects on her feelings.

Box 5.1: Mrs. Lerner's Reflection

I am feeling nervous that someone (the author) is watching the class. I want my students to show how well they can perform. I'm also anxious, wanting the students to be able to show their capabilities with an observer present. To overcome this anxiety, I'm going to carefully use my own emotional information to stay closely "in touch" with non-verbal cues in case one of my students has something important to say.

Following her quick self-reflection, Mrs. Lerner focuses her attention on her class. After directing the students to listen carefully, she asks them to talk about the feelings of characters in books they are reading—speaking as if they are the character:

- "I feel bad because I don't like to play the violin and I'm forced to do it."
- "I feel guilty because I wasn't going to play."
- "I feel sad because I can't afford a pony." Here Mrs. Lerner asks if the pony is the real reason for being sad. The student contin ues, "the problem is that I have no friends and then I become sad because I can't afford a pony for a friend."

Both mainstream and special education students eagerly discuss their feelings. All students appear to be comfortable chatting about the book, yet are aware that Mrs. Lerner is teaching one of the basic skills of Social Decision-Making: identify the feelings underlying a problem before identifying the actual problem, possible solutions and their conse- quences.

Mrs. Lerner then proceeds to read the book, which is about a Vietnamese student named Ut who moves to the United States and goes to an American School. Dressed in Vietnamese attire, which appears like pajamas, Ut is laughed at by the other students.

"How does Ut feel about this?" Mrs. Lerner asks the class.

"He feels sad and angry," replies one of her students, and the class talks about how it is possible to feel two feelings at the same time.

Later in the story, Ut and another student get into a fight. Just as the principal appears in the story, Mrs. Lerner closes the book and asks the students to step into character.

"How does the principal feel?" she asks.

The class responds, "Mad. Angry. Disappointed. Surprised. Sad. Upset."

Mrs. Lerner then asks the students to describe the problem under- lying his feelings. One student says, "To get the students to stop fighting."

Mrs. Lerner asks the class to develop a number of solutions for the principal to use to get the students to stop fighting, and to describe the consequences of each solution. After being reminded to listen carefully and speak one at a time, the students continue with possible answers:

- "Call the parents. The consequence might be that both students get grounded. It doesn't solve the problem because the kids will get more angry at each other and fight back again."

- "Give detention. It could stop the fighting, but might not."
- "Suspend them. The kids think it's fun not to have to go to school. It won't stop the fighting necessarily."
- "Separate them all the time by never letting them have recess at the same time. This might stop the fighting."
- "Get them together and let them talk it out. This has a good chance of stopping the fighting because they might become better friends. It also has risks that they might get madder."

Next, Mrs. Lerner asks the class to vote on the best solution. Seven students want to let the students talk it out. Four prefer calling their parents. No one selects detention or suspension. Mrs. Lerner then returns to the book and lets them see that the book chose the same alternative they did: to talk the problem out. (If the book had a different outcome, she would note that there is often more than one way to solve a problem.) The period ends with Mrs. Lerner telling the class to read the rest of the book on their own. Mrs. Lerner turns her attention to herself for a moment:

Box 5.3: Mrs. Lerner's Reflection

I'm so proud of my students. I've never asked my students to identify with the principal in a story before. I always asked them to identify with other students. Now I've found a new way to teach empathy by asking the students to see the world from a teacher's perspective. And all the kids did this so easily.

After class Mrs. Lerner explains to me how effective this approach has been in developing the critical thinking skills of the special needs children: "Brainstorming feeling words helps them to expand their vocabulary. Understanding then feelings of others leads to alternative ways to analyze a problem. Listening to the solutions of the other children gives them the opportunity to stretch their ideas."

In addition to using "feeling" words as problem-solving tools, Mrs. Lerner's students explore alternative solutions and their consequences. And by modeling the regular education children, the special education students develop the confidence to go out on the playground with them— which before practice in emotional learning was not possible.

Developing Basic Skills

The basic skills that students are taught include a simple but powerful behavioral approach to recognizing feelings and learning to process them (Elias, M. and Clabby, J. 1979). Posters describing each of the skills are displayed prominently in every classroom at Bartle, enjoining students to focus their attention on their feelings and physical sensations—the first step in becoming self-aware (see Exhibits 5.1-5.3, at the end of this chapter).

Teachers will use these directions regularly and model them for students in the classroom. For example, a teacher might share with her students that she was able to stay relaxed during a traffic bottleneck by telling herself to "keep calm," regulating her breath, relaxing and centering herself through a "self-talk" strategy. By practicing and modeling these skills regularly in the classroom from kindergarten onward, teachers help students to relax even in the most stressful situations.

Using Self-Awareness Skills with Classroom Management

All the teachers in the Bartle School use basic skills of emotional awareness for classroom management. This is evident in the fourth-grade social studies class, where the children are studying immigration after a trip to Ellis Island. Today, the children are sitting across from one another at four large tables. Each child has a sign that identifies the nationality they have chosen from a book they are reading. In this highly diverse classroom, an African-American girl's sign reads "Greek;" a Chinese boy's sign says "African;" and a Mexican child's sign reads "Japanese."

The class explores why different national groups immigrated to the United States. The African-American boy whose sign reads "Jewish" explains, "My father was beaten up because we were Jews." The Mexican boy whose sign reads "Greek" explains, "We came to make more money."

This is a class topic that can easily become overly animated and emotional. Yet at various points of the discussion, the teacher brings the whole class back to calm with a simple statement: "Keep Calm/Listening Skills." Hearing this direction for a basic skill, the whole class becomes centered and quiet. By turning the children's attention to their thoughts and their feelings about immigration, the teacher helps the students develop empathy as well as explore the similarities and differences of their ancestors.

Difficulty Learning Emotional Awareness Skills

When a student has difficulty learning an emotional awareness skill, he or she will go (or be asked by the teacher to go) to a special area of the classroom. Here the child will have access to worksheets and materials (see below on the Problem Diary) that will help in exploring the underlying feelings that are blocking the ability to utilize the skill effectively.

Teacher or parent can refer those who are consistently unable to learn the skill to the Social Decision-Making Lab for a 30-40 minute individual skill-building session once a week. (See Social Decision-Making Lab below.)

Learning Emotional Awareness Skills is Difficult

While emotional awareness skills are simple, learning to access them in stressful moments can be difficult. One seventh grader tells a story about how hard it was to remember "Keep Calm" when he was getting baited into a fight. Through classroom activities that helped him to become aware of what his physical signs of stress were, he learned that when he became angry he always put his hands in his pocket. He used this self-knowledge to problem solve, and created a card for his pocket with the "Keep Calm" instructions, thus developing his own learning accommodations. He explained, "The card (which he has laminated) says 'Keep Calm' and 'Slow Down' on the front, and 'Think before you action'(his phrase) on the back. You cannot think if you do not slow down first."

This boy also expressed his frustration when he learned two different approaches to "Keep Calm," one in a drug class and the other in a bullying class. While they were essentially the same, each approach recommended a different count for holding your breath. "I was angry and I just didn't know which to choose so I hit the guy who was bothering me, said the boy." This example offers an important lesson for teachers: only through a standard skills curriculum that runs through every class in the school can we expect children to understand and learn emotional awareness skills effectively.

Teaching Basic Skills in Health Class

Because she is regularly in contact with students across grade levels, the guidance counselor gets to know all the students. While the health class is normally taught by the health teacher, today guidance counselor Vicky Poedubicky teaches the health class to take the pulse of fourth graders. This class is designed to help students recognize and describe different feelings using "Feelings Bingo" (see Exhibit 5.4, at the end of this chapter).

Mrs. Poedubicky begins by handing out blank Bingo cards and writing a list of words on the board. She tells the students to pick the words they would like to include in their Bingo Chart and write them in. One little girl comments to the girl in the next seat, "I've experienced all the feelings in the first list. I'm going to pick all new feeling words today so that I can experience something new."

When the students have finished setting up their boards, Mrs. Poedubicky begins drawing words from her box. She says, "Listening Position" and all eyes come to attention on her as she picks 'annoyed' and uses the word in a sentence: " I get annoyed when I try to talk and others don't listen." This is the rule of the game: You must use the word picked in a sentence. "Put a word with how you feel."

After she completes the first five examples, Mrs. Poedubicky lets students make up the sentences. The attention of the class moves from their Bingo Cards to the experience of feelings. Mrs. Poedubicky moves to exploring the emotional awareness skills needed to handle the feeling states. "I have a set of skills in my belt. Which one do I need when I get **annoyed?**"

Hands go up slowly and the children mention "Keep Calm, " "Speaker Power" and "Problem Diary." They talk about how to use these tools to handle being annoyed.

When the bell rings, the students have long since forgotten about the Bingo game and are leaving class discussing the nuance of their feelings. Mrs. Poedubicky takes the moment after the class to reflect:

Box 5.4 Mrs. Poedubicky' Self-Reflection

I'm somewhat disappointed with the class. Although the spirit of the class was high, the children were slow to acquire the core emotional awareness skills. When I conduct future professional development sessions, I know now that I must stress more practice time for students.

By integrating emotional awareness skills into the academic curriculum, teachers can expand the critical thinking skills of their students. Here a second part of the basic behavioral training becomes important: *FIGTESPN* (Elias and Tobias, 1996), a framework for reflecting on one's feelings by understanding how best to act on them. The framework (Exhibit5.5, at the end of this chapter) includes eight steps:

- **F**eelings need to be recognized at that moment.
- **I**dentify the underlying issues relating to the feelings.
- **G**uide yourself with a goal.
- **T**hink of many possible alternatives to reaching your goal.
- **E**nvision end results for each option.
- **S**elect your best option.
- **P**lan the procedure and anticipate roadblocks.
- **N**otice what happened and remember it for next time.

By third grade, students are expected to be able to recognize and describe the feelings they are having inside themselves. They are taught in their health class to use the correct vocabulary to describe different feeling states. They are expected to be able to describe the "FIG" of any situation (Recognize the **F**eeling; **I**dentify the problem behind the feeling; **G**uide yourself to a goal and contemplate what you would like to happen.) By fifth grade they will learn to use the entire model.

Using FIGTESPN in a Fifth Grade Literature Class

In Mrs. Denelle Lahr Kagan's fifth grade literature class, the students are using FIGTESPN as a framework for understanding the central feelings, potential actions, and consequences of these actions for a character from the literature they are studying, *Gilly Hopkins* by Katherine Paterson. Before starting the class, Mrs. Kagan momentarily turns her attention to herself:

Box 5.5: Mrs. Kagan's Self-Reflection

I'm both nervous and happy having the students apply *FIGTESPN* to their literature analysis for the first time. I'll handle my anxiety by being extra careful in giving direction for the assignment.

Mrs. Kagan separates the class into five groups of three to four students each. After reading a chapter from the book, the groups are instructed to pretend they are the main character, Gilly, and write down a sequence of possible action she can take to respond to what she is feeling following the decision framework of *FIGTESPN*.

The students are busily discussing Gilly's problem, which one student articulates after 15 minutes of shared discussion: "I feel angry and desperate because I need $100 to buy a bus ticket (**F**eeling). The issue behind my anger is that I don't have enough money (**I**ssue). My goal is to get the money I need (**G**uide). The way I think I could get the money is either to earn it or steal it (**T**hink). The result of stealing the money would be I could end up in jail, but working to earn the money would take a lot of time (**E**nvision)."

The group spends a lot of time trying to come up with a number of alternatives until the class period ends, and Mrs. Kagan tells the class to read the next Chapter of *Gilly Hopkins* to develop more information for their decision framework. Mrs. Kagan takes a moment to reflect on the class before moving to the next subject:

> Box 4.6: Mrs. Kagan's Self-Reflection
>
> I feel very excited! The class went well, as the students were able to easily apply the FIGTESPN model to Gilly. I remember how important these emotional awareness-building skills were to my comfort level as a new teacher. The skills particularly helped me to deal with my more oppositional students by guiding them to more effectively attend to the class.

After class Mrs. Kagan is enthusiastic in talking with me about her experience in working with Bartle's emotional learning program:

As a new teacher last year I was really surprised at the degree of emotional information the children are able to access. I had five students in my class who were struggling with oppositional behavior. By working with these students to help them understand the feelings that led to their being inattentive, they were able to make great headway in handling their problems and become more attentive classroom participants. We all benefited.

Using the Problem Diary

The *Problem Diary* (see Exhibit 5.6), introduced to students in third grade, is a self-directed method often used to help students identify the feelings that get in the way of their classroom attention. It is available in every classroom to help the student sort through feelings and re-evaluate the situation. A teacher can direct a student to fill out a Problem Diary when self-awareness may be the key to enabling the student to gain self-control. Such situations include:

- Exhibiting behavioral problems in the classroom, such as hitting, stealing, or getting out of one's seat inappropriately;
- Failing to complete assignments;
- Getting into confrontations with another student;
- Having personal problems within the family or peer group;
- Being distracted or inattentive;
- Demonstrating a lack of respect toward the teacher;
- Using verbal outbursts occur such as blurting out, name-calling or arguing.

Filling out a Problem Diary may be sufficient to get to the feelings that will help resolve a problem. For those students who need additional help, the teacher may make a referral to the Social Problem Solving Lab, described below.

The Social Problem Solving Lab

The lab is a place where students can gain self-awareness and understanding of how feelings are getting in the way of learning. Students can refer themselves to the lab, or can be referred by a parent or teacher. It is not only for "problem" students, but for any student who wants to better communicate with others and express feelings in productive ways. A student referred to the lab usually spends one 40-minute period a week working on skill building with a guidance counselor, health teacher, student intern, or alone working on the computer. The lab leader will also inform teachers about all skills taught to a student in the lab, so that the lab can become an integral part of the student's curriculum.

Guidance Counselor Poedubicky tells of a girl named Patty, who was referred to the Problem Solving Lab by her teacher after a great deal of difficulty controlling her blurting out behavior in her fifth grade class. Completing a Problem Diary, meeting with interns, and working on the computer, Patty explored the reasons behind her distractedness. She had many complex, anxiety producing things going on in her life, which she needed to sort out.

By working in the lab at her own initiative for the rest of the semester, Patty learned to understand and better manage her feelings so she could control her classroom outbursts. Patty regularly reported her activities back to her class. Her teacher recognized that Patty took great pride in her lab work, which she shared with others in the class who were doing parallel work using the FIGTESPN model. Importantly, her attendance at the lab did not make Patty feel isolated—it brought her back to the class with expertise to share.

A guidance counselor or intern is usually available to work with a student to explore where he or she has difficulty identifying the feelings that are getting in the way of his or her school performance. Other tools are available include Feeling Face Cards, which display different faces expressing a wide variety of feelings, and finger-paints for drawing a Feelings Fingerprint (See Exhibit 5.7, at the end of this chapter)—a tracing of hand or finger that introduces a discussion of how a person's feelings sometimes manifest through a physical, bodily response.

When a student first visits the lab, a plan is laid out to define what is to be worked on, and to review over time whether skills previously introduced were helpful to the student. In addition, the referring teacher must be notified about what was covered in the lab, thereby making the lab an integral part of the student's curriculum.

Integrating Self-Awareness and Discipline

Emotional awareness has become a big part of the discipline system at Bartle. When a student does something that requires discipline, teachers and administrators first look at the role of emotion in the situation. The student immediately fills out a Problem Diary. In this way the student has a chance to identify the underlying feeling that led to the poor judgment.

Counselor Poedubicky describes one situation:

> We had two sixth grade boys receive an in-school suspension consequence for "making a poor choice." We decided to try having the boys work in the Social Decision Making Lab assisting kids with solving problems or making decisions. Using the computer software program, as well as other strategies, they helped student after student all day. They also accompanied me to a third grade health class to help teach emotional awareness skills. No, it wasn't a conventional "in-school suspension," but they spent the day problem solving and thinking of ways to help third grade students think clearly. I will keep tabs on these sixth grade boys to see if their experience causes them to reflect when in a stressful situation.

Whenever possible, Bartle teachers and administrators try to help students recognize the underlying feelings behind the discipline situation, and have students resolve the true cause of the problem. This practice provides balance to the negative consequences that students experience when they make poor decisions, and helps them avoid the disciplinary action in the future.

Bartle is an exciting example of the difference that emotional awareness can make in the learning process of a school, a teacher and a student. The strength of the system is best expressed by the enthusiasm and confidence of the Bartle teachers.

Exhibit 5.1

Keep Calm

Keep Calm is something that will help you solve problems and handle your trigger situations. There are four simple things to remember:

1.   Tell yourself, **"STOP AND TAKE A LOOK AROUND."**

2.   Tell yourself, **"KEEP CALM."**

3.   Take a deep breath through your nose while you count to five, hold it while you count to two, then breath out through your mouth while you count to five.

4.   Repeat these steps until you feel calm.

Exhibit 5.2

Be Your BEST

BODY POSTURE

Standing up straight,
being confident in yourself
but not arrogant.

EYE CONTACT

Looking the person
directly in the eye,
communicating openly.

SPEECH

Using nice words, and
saying what you really
feel.

TONE OF VOICE

Using a calm voice, not
whispering or shouting.

Exhibit 5.3

Listening Position

1)   Sit or stand straight.

2)   Face the speaker.

3)   Look at the speaker or source of the subject.

Exhibit 5.4

Feelings Bingo

Embarrassed	Hopeful	Calm	Depressed
Friendly	Loved	Tense	Confident
Feelings	Nervous	Mad	Fantastic
Happy	Angry	Troubled	Relieved
Confused	Surprised	Scared	Anxious
Terrific	Disappointed	Hurt	Forceful
Annoyed	Curious	Joyful	Comfortable
Envious	Terrific	Jealous	Sad

Exhibit 5.5

How to Act on Feelings

FIGTESPN

- **F**eelings need to be recognized at that moment.

- **I**dentify the underlying issues that relate to the feelings.

- **G**uide yourself with a goal.

- **T**hink of many possible alternatives to reaching your goal.

- **E**nvision end results for each option.

- **S**elect your best option.

- **P**lan the procedure and anticipate roadblocks.

- **N**otice what happened and remember it for next time.

Exhibit 5.6

Problem Diary

Name: _____   Date: _____

My feelings look like this:

I am feeling

_____

_____

_____

_____

_____

[ ]

Tell the Problem
What did you say and do?   Draw it...

_____

_____

_____

_____

_____

_____

[ ]

Now what do you wnat to have happen?   Draw it...

_____

_____

_____

_____

[ ]

What things could you do to make it
happen?   Draw it...

_____

_____

_____

_____

_____

_____

[ ]

Exhibit 5.7

Feelings Fingerprint

Put your fingerprints here.

_____   _____   _____

What do your fingerprints look like?

_____
_____
_____
_____
_____

Write your feelings here.

It feels like this... _____
_____
_____

It feels like this... _____
_____
_____

It feels like this... _____
_____
_____

6
Accessing Emotional Information

Emotional information is the moment-to-moment meaning-making we understand from the experience of our feelings, emotions, physical body sensations and emotional memories. In contrast to our thoughts and ideas, which are often cognitively developed through logic and applied principle, emotional information is, by its nature, personal and subjective. Yet as we have pointed out in previous chapters, emotional information constantly unconsciously informs our learning and teaching—whether we choose to pay attention to it or not. When we choose to consciously access and understand it, we can better comprehend how emotional information influences our ultimate choices and judgments. The educational goal then is to enable students to be aware of their emotional information, and to make choices about how it will impact their decision-making.

In Chapter 5 we introduced the basic skill "stay calm," which is one method for helping students learn to access their emotional information. We will now consider other methods for accessing emotional information, first with adolescents and then with five-year-olds.

Box 6.1: Author Reflection (Claudia)

I find that as adolescents move through the day, they are often emotionally charged and experience a whole range of physical stress signs: stomach or head pain, tight muscles, and irritability. They, like most of us, learn to tune out these signs and try to focus on the task at hand. Or, they just "tune out" entirely and ignore what is happening around them. Either of these techniques can make students unfocused or disruptive. To get to the root of the problem, I began doing the "relax" exercise with students in my classes a couple of times a week—with wonderful results. Students were better able to concentrate, and overall appeared more centered and calm. They listened more closely and were more balanced in expressing their viewpoints. We all felt better as a result.

Now let's visit Mrs. Olsen's seventh grade class where students are learning the "Relax" skill. She explains the "Relax" exercise to her class as a visualization technique used by athletes and others who want to maximize their performance. She tells them that by visualizing something in your mind, your brain believes you are actually doing the activity, and the body responds accordingly.

The first time students practice "Relax," Mrs. Olsen talks them through the process. She then uses the same instructions for the rest of the year. The "Relax" process has three steps. (Teachers who are not as comfortable with the exercise as described here can use a relaxation visualization tape if they prefer.)

Step 1. Have students sit in a comfortable position with their eyes closed and their attention focused on their breathing. Slowly ask them to follow your voice as you direct them to relax each part of the body while slowly breathing in and out: feet, legs, stomach, shoulders, arms, fingers, head, face. (The sequence and words used to instruct students should remain the same each time they practice the exercise.)

Step 2. Ask the students to go to a special place of their own creation in their imaginations. Tell them to bring whatever people or things they would like to feel even more relaxed. Assure them that no one else can have access to this place without their permission.

Step 3. Tell the students they can stay in their imaginary place for a moment, but must then come back into the room. Let them know they can return to their special havens any time they wish. Also encourage students to jot down their experience during the exercise in their journals for later reference.

Mrs. Olsen usually practices this exercise at least once a week with her entire class. Sometimes she will ask the students in their relaxed state to imagine a situation in which they might be vulnerable to using drugs or alcohol or abusing food, or to imagine what it would feel like to be a bully or a victim in a situation. She then asks them to imagine how they would respond to this situation, and to record this information in a journal they keep. Mrs. Olsen finds that journaling helps the students integrate their personal reactions before sharing their thoughts with others. In this way, the class discussion becomes richer and more meaningful.

For example, one day in class discussion, Mrs. Olson asked students how they would respond to offers of alcohol or drugs at a party. The students quickly said they would just say "no." She then did the Relax exercise, and asked the students the same question. After they had recorded their individual experiences in their journals, the class discussed the topic again. This time, the students had gathered much emotional information about the subject. In their relaxed states, they felt the realities of peer pressures, and not wanting to look like a geek. Saying "no" was not as simple as they originally thought. The class discussion following the exercise became significantly more intense as students shared genuine concerns and debated practical solutions.

Whatever the question, student answers are much more realistic and serious after the Relax exercise. This is because students are accessing their emotional information in addition to their thoughts. Together with keeping a journal, the "Relax" exercise can help students really recognize the feelings behind issues. In the beginning, some members of the class may find the exercise a little awkward; with practice, however, they will find that they are able to quickly relax, get in touch with their feelings, and explore the issues on their minds.

Box 6.2: Mrs. Olsen's Reflection

"Relax" helps students get directly in touch with the feeling state in which they could be vulnerable to destructive behavior. I find that once they are in this place, they can work backward in the sequence to recognize early warning signs that they might be headed for trouble, and develop a plan for avoiding the ultimate negative consequence. Students who have difficulty mastering "Relax" are students I need to pay attention to. Those who do not master the skill are often the students who are later referred for problem behaviors because they have not found constructive ways to handle disturbing feelings.

Using "Relax" in Other Classes

Teachers who have not experienced guided relaxation before may find the experience of teaching it a little awkward. However, this usually disappears with practice. Many teachers create their own tape recording of themselves leading the exercise, so they can repeat it in the same way in each class session. Mrs. Hidalgo is a seventh grade math teacher who learned the technique at a professional development program in her school, and has effectively adapted it to increase student performance in math.

Mrs. Hidalgo has a student named Jon who is having difficulty in her math class. He has demonstrated strong math aptitudes on IQ tests, so she's not sure what is interfering with Jon's performance in class except that he appears very anxious. If she asks Jon direct questions, he only becomes more anxious and totally withdraws from the class. Mrs.

Hidalgo decides that she needs to indirectly facilitate conversations with Jon that support both of them in using their emotional information to explore clues to the source of his math difficulties.

Mrs. Hidalgo decides to conduct a classroom exercise for all students. During math she initiates the Relax exercise in which the students close their eyes and reflect on themselves. She asks them to imagine any concerns, problems or issues that could block their best performance in math, and then to open their eyes and record what they imagined on a piece of paper. All the students busily write down their answers. After completing the Relax exercise, Mrs. Hidalgo asks the students to share any of their concerns. While Jon does not join in the discussion, he hears many of the students share the anxieties they sometimes feel in math. Mrs. Hidalgo then passes out little paper boxes into which the students can put their written "math blockers." She tells the class that during the term, they are all going to work to "empty their worry boxes" by developing strategies to overcome their concerns. She also collects the boxes from the students and tells them she would like to review their individual concerns, but will return the boxes for their use in future math classes.

This exercise allowed Mrs. Hidalgo to explore the emotional information of her students. She learned from reviewing Jon's "math blockers" that he has feelings of anxiety over being unable to read the board. He also fears that he may be called upon to answer a question, because he is uncomfortable speaking in front of large groups. She has now found a way to broach the subject with Jon in a direct discussion.

Mrs. Hidalgo learns that before the class exercise Jon felt he was the only one in the class who felt anxious, and he really didn't understand the source of his anxiety. The Relax exercise helped him identify the cause. In addition, by hearing the responses of his classmates, he realized that feeling some anxiety is perfectly normal. He also saw talking with Mrs. Hidalgo about the problem as a normal part of the classroom exercise. He was ready when she approached him directly to discuss how a seat adjustment might solve his board-reading problem, and how some public-speaking practice might make him comfortable speaking in front of the class.

The exercise also helped Mrs. Hidalgo reduce the level of anxiety she feels when she presents a math lesson that the students have difficulty understanding. By understanding the concerns raised by the students in their worry boxes, Mrs. Hidalgo knows that she needs to attend to the emotional side of teaching math as well as the mechanics of the mathematics lessons.

Box 6.3: Author Self-Reflection (Claudia)

I have used the Relax exercise many times with students over the years, and have found that it is an extremely powerful technique for helping students learn more effectively. For example, in classes where I have used it before exams, I have found that average test scores are as much as 10% higher than in classes without it. In addition, students are able to focus more clearly and organize their thoughts more effectively after the exercise. Stress levels come down after regular practice of the exercise. Student voices take a lower pitch, and concentration levels immediately improve. In one class where the students urged me to practice the exercise twice weekly, the students asked at the end of the term, "Mrs. Shelton, could you start a new school where we could do Relax everyday. It is just so helpful." It may be a little awkward for teachers and students to learn the skill in the beginning, but it is well worth the effort.

Feelings and Physical Sensations

Another subject important to understanding emotional information is related to physical body sensations. Emotional reactions to different situations are reflected in, and often signaled by, physical sensations. Moreover, students may have certain common ways of expressing emotion through body posture, positions, gestures and sensations. Being well acquainted with these body correlates is very helpful for self-knowledge and equally helpful for teachers who may sometimes listen to complaints about physical ailments.

Learning about the relation between physical body sensation and feelings is the subject of this next lesson. Let's stop at Ms. Christina's pre-K classroom to observe a lesson on feelings in our bodies. Ms. Christina asks her five year olds: "Who can recognize feelings in their bodies? In what parts of your body do you have these feelings?"

Students raise their hands and participate in a lively discussion about butterflies in the stomach, headaches, and sweaty palms. Ms. Christina then passes out to each student the outline of a body. She asks each student to color in the different parts of the body where they have feelings, using different color crayons to represent different feelings. After that, Ms. Christina asks the students to work with their table partner and tell a story about a time that a particular part of the body let them know that they were having a particular feeling. The students actively tell their stories to their partners.

Box 6.4: Ms. Christina's Self-Reflection

I always enjoy watching these youngsters get connected with their bodies. It allows me the opportunity to reinforce the benefits of exercise and physical energy. It also reminds me to pay attention to my own reactions! So many times my stomach lets me know that something is troubling me, even if I can't quite put my finger on it. I am also reminded that while there are may similarities between one stomach ache and another, in terms of feelings like nervousness or excitement, there are also many different patterns of students' reactions to their stomachs. I look forward to my students being able to tell me more about this!

It is easy to imagine using a variation of this lesson in other classrooms, for older students. For example, create a matching exercise by listing feeling and emotion-related words such as embarrassed, stressed, happy, nervous on one side of the page, and a body outline on the other. The more students recognize the link between their physical body sensations and their feelings, the more they can be aware of sensations that predict emotional states, and the more they can understand what to do to manage their feelings.

Each student will have his or her unique set of physical responses and behaviors that accompany these reactions. Recognizing this connection allows teachers to observe emotions in students before they are reported, or when students ignore these sensations themselves.

Box 6.5: Author Reflection (Robin)

I like this lesson a lot. I think it is an easy, pictorial way of helping students make the link between heart, mind and body! I have seen teachers from pre-K to tenth grade engage their students in thinking about and talking about the physical sensations that accompany feelings. I think it is very valuable to note and to share with students the awareness that it is not only fear and excitement that are expressed physically—all of our emotions have physical correlates. The more we know about our own bodies, and our own patterns of reactions (just as Ms. Christina reflected on above) the more control we have over our behavior in response to our feelings, and the more information we have about our response to the happenings in our everyday lives.

7
Differentiating Sources of Stress

Teachers and students face work that can be extremely stressful at times. The mix of lessons, hectic schedules, exams, deadlines, and extra-curricular commitments all can lead to burn-out when not managed effectively. We can all learn to handle stress, but each of us experiences and manages it differently. Sometimes we even create our own stresses as we hold on to behaviors that feel comfortable, but are not supportive of our current goals and objectives. Chapter 7 helps to identify these different stress patterns, and the warning signs that both teachers and students can learn to recognize to know when to shift from a behavior that reinforces negative stress patterns.

Think for a moment about how you handle stress, following Box 7.1.

Box 7.1: Self-Talk Exercise

How do I recognize when my students are experiencing stress? Does stress seem to be beneficial for some students, and not for others? How can I help students recognize early signs of stress so that they can change their behavior to more constructive ways of behaving? How important is stress management to my overall classroom management? How do I experience stress? What is it that puts me into a stressful set of behavior patterns that can be self-defeating? What signs do I recognize in myself that mean it's time to re-group?

Many psychologists, counselors, and researchers have written about the importance of having a clear mental objective for any task (Leider, 1997, & Seligman, 1995). A statement of strategy or mission helps focus attention and energy on the tasks that need to be accomplished to achieve a goal. Yet the instinctive social-emotional path an individual takes to reach that goal may sometimes work against the rational objective. In Chapter 7, we refer to "Know your Emotional Purpose," which is a framework that helps individuals understand not only their objective path toward goals, but also the instinctive emotional stressors they are unintentionally including in their goal-seeking behavior patterns.

Box 7.2: Author Reflection (Claudia)

I developed the "Know Your Emotional Purpose" framework and exercise after working with many students and teachers who were extremely goal-oriented but had difficulty reaching their goals. Emotion contributes greatly to our goal orientation, for better or for worse, and I have found that it helps to identify the "emotional path" of our goals as well as the rational path.

Let's consider an example. Manuel wants to get into a good college and is doing everything he can to make his application attractive. His instinctive emotional reaction is to join many school clubs and sports teams, work outside of school, do community service, and get involved in a myriad of other activities. He rationalizes his feelings with an "instinctive belief" that by showing how many things he does, he will get a favorable response to his application. Unfortunately, he overloads himself with so many activities that he starts letting things drop and doesn't finish anything very well. Manuel reveals a typical stress pattern of many high achievers.

As he recognizes this self-induced stress pattern as potentially destructive, Manuel re-examines his instinctive reaction of taking on so many activities. He may also reconsider his belief that more activities lead to a more favorable college response. His revised stress management strategy will involve being more selective in what he does, thus both lowering his stress and doing a better job on the things he selects to do. Through this self-examination of the source of his negative stress, he will ultimately be able to articulate his choices more effectively in his college application, rather than appearing as a Jack-of-all-trades and master of none.

The process for "Knowing Your Emotional Purpose" involves three steps:

Step 1. Identify the instinctive emotional patterns through which you recognize stressful and secure behaviors in yourself. (Nine different patterns will be described in detail in the classroom exercise that follows.) For some students, stress may be exhibited as overly aggressive, in-your-face behavior. For others, it may manifest as extreme withdrawal.

Manuel's pattern is that when he wants someone to like him (e.g. a college to accept him) he tries to impress them by doing many activities.

Step 2. Through self-reflective observation, notice when and how your instinctive emotional pattern pushes you toward destructive stress as you try to accomplish your goal. Manuel, for example, needs to realize that he is moving into negative stress whenever he takes on more activities than he can successfully manage.

Step 3. Use self-talk to help yourself modify your behavior and move toward a more constructive, secure emotional pattern. Some students set up a buddy system to keep each other posted about the stressful behavior they notice in one another and to note when a behavior change is necessary. In Manuel's case, when he gets too busy and misses deadlines he realizes that he needs to reorganize his schedule and tells himself to drop several activities so that he can to effectively meet his commitments again.

The Enneagram

Different people exhibit different patterns of experiencing stress, and they find many different ways to change their behavior for the better. The Enneagram is a self-reflective model that can be helpful in understanding underlying stressors. We don't know the exact origin of the Enneagram. We do know that it was used by ancient tribes like the Sufi Indians in South America as a rite of passage for adolescents to understand the adult role they are naturally gifted to play the community. In ancient tribes, information from the Enneagram was considered "sacred knowledge" that only the leaders of the community could personally communicate. The model was discovered by missionaries working with the Sufi Indians, and brought to the United States for eventual publication. Stanford University held the first international Enneagram conference several years ago.

The Enneagram model is now used in diverse settings including education, career counseling, and corporate leadership development. Educator Janet Levine has been a leader in teaching the Enneagram to teachers around the world. She clearly sees the benefits to teachers who learn this system (Levine, 1999). They are better able to express in words what we sometimes call "chemistry" between people. Teachers learn to be more aware of their teaching process, and of the ways in which they shift between conditions of stress and security; they can use this knowledge to more effectively manage classroom pressure.

Box 7.3: Author Self-Reflection (Claudia)

Learning the Enneagram takes a little work, but it is worth the effort. I have used it with teachers, students and administrators, who want to see the emotional blind spots that may hold them back. To quickly understand the potential of this system, I recommend you purchase *Discovering Your Personality Type* by Don Richard Riso, which is available in most bookstores. It has a questionnaire, which lets you try the model out on yourself to see what it tells you about unintentional patterns that create stress in your life.

I have taught ninth graders about the Enneagram for five years in a 10-session course. It is a remarkable experience, in which I see my students build a tremendous understanding about one another. For example, one student recognized that his learning problems were much less related to attention deficit than to his instinctive stress patterns, which he could control. Recently, I have met many high school English teachers who are incorporating, with great results, the teaching of the Enneagram into analysis of the characters in the books their class reads.

The Enneagram model includes a set of nine distinct archetypal personalities, called "points," each one with a particular central theme. The Enneagram is usually illustrated (see Exhibit 7.1, at the end of this chapter) by a diagram of triangles within a circle with each point identified on the circumference of the circle by a number from 1 to 9. The arrow moving away from the point is the stress point, while the arrow moving toward the point is the point of security.

The central theme or story of each archetype is briefly summarized in Exhibit 7.2 (found at the end of this chapter).

Exhibit 7.3, (found at the end of this chapter), summarizes the stress and secure behaviors associated with each of the 9 points. Let's consider Manuel's story again by viewing Exhibit 7.2 and 7.3 to see how the Enneagram works.

Through classroom discussion and completing the Riso questionnaire, Manuel has identified himself as most often acting like a Point 3. Looking at Exhibit 7.2, we see that the Point 3 is interested in accomplishing or achieving things so that people feel good about him. In Exhibit 7.3, we see that under stress Manuel will likely exhibit negative qualities of the Point 9 archetype such as getting overloaded, forgetting his original reason for getting involved in the task, and feeling anxious. To reduce his stress, Manuel needs to move toward his secure archetype, Point 6. The positive qualities of Point 6, such as setting priorities and clarifying organization, will move Manuel back toward feeling secure.

The Enneagram is almost like a slowly unfolding mystery that students just can't wait to solve. Ninth and tenth graders find this a helpful way of gaining perspective on their behavior, -especially when under stress. At times each of us acts like all of the 9 Points, but we usually relate especially well to one or two of the archetypes.

We urge you to explore the books listed in the bibliography to better understand the teaching and learning power of this system. Janet Levine's *The Enneagram Intelligences* (2001) was written specifically for educators. It provides detailed information for teachers who want to become more aware of their own behavior in the classroom.

Using the Enneagram in the Classroom

The tenth grade Human Growth and Development course about the Enneagram is taught by Ms. Marshall in 10 class sessions. During the first class, students are introduced to Enneagram study using Rene Baron and Elizabeth Wegerle's *Enneagram Made Easy* textbook (1994). Students also self-administer the Riso-Hudson Enneagram questionnaire from the book *Discovering Your Personality Type* (Riso, 1995). Ms. Marshall explains to her students:

> We are trying to build self-awareness, not trying to "type" people. The Enneagram provides an engaging, thought-provoking and fun way to do this. What's also important is the discipline it will give you to guide your own reflective process about yourself and your friends.

The perceived safety of the environment is probably the most important factor for the success of the class. Students must always be made to feel comfortable discussing their personal observations of one another. Teachers must define the boundary between interpersonal questions and intimate, personal questions. This is a tough lesson and takes good modeling skills by the teacher. We want to share information that helps us understand how we can work better together when we realize our differences, not probe into people's personal lives or share potentially embarrassing secrets about each other. Ms. Marshall is reflective before she approaches her class, as described in Box 7.3.

Within the safe environment, students are comfortable sharing their personal feelings. For example, one boy explains:

> Under stress I will get very icy and will get my adrenalin going, which makes me very aggressive, but this will only be for a short period of time and then I start work on solving the problem. If it is something like sports, I will take my aggression out on the other team's players while staying within the rules of the game.

Establishing a Class Format

In each class, Enneagram Points are explored using Janet Levine's student video, *Nine Perspectives on What Motivates Learning in Adolescents* (Levine, 1995). The video has three-minute segments of a high school student reflecting on each of the Enneagram points. Class discussion focuses on how the featured student sees the world, experiences stress, and how that stress can be changed into secure confidence. The segment allows the class to "walk in the world" of each Enneagram archetype.

Each day as the class studies a different Enneagram Point, the video segment for that point is viewed. Following the video, the teacher informally interviews the student(s) in the classroom, who believe this Point represents their perspective, while the rest of the class listens. This allows the teacher to model questioning behavior. After three to five minutes, the other students in the class can ask questions of the expert student(s).

Usually, the teacher will give the students a homework assignment that requires them to think about the Enneagram archetype studied on that day. The objective is to get them to reflect on emotional patterns of behavior. An assignment might ask the students to identify teachers or celebrities whom they believe represent a certain archetype; the students are then required to back up their responses with appropriate evidence. Another assignment might require the students to interview family members or friends who represent the point being studied.

Ms. Marshall's class is a graded course that culminates with a term paper in which students identify an aspect of their behavior that they would like to study using the Enneagram. The students gather data about themselves through self-reflection as well as through interviews with friends, teachers, and family members. They document their conclusions about the underlying patterns of their behavior in relation to friends, family, potential career, handling of stress, and perceived purpose in life. Ms. Marshall is very clear about her method of grading the paper.

Students are able to distinguish how applying a psychological model is similar to applying any other model we use to study math or history. The Enneagram model is only a map describing certain aspects of personal dynamics so we can objectively talk about ourselves with other people and get feedback. This is a sophisticated skill. The course grade is a result of how well students use the model to explore, not their ability to identify their "type." Thoughtful information gathering goes to the heart of self-reflective skill building.

Box 7.4 shows that Ms. Marshall was initially anxious about her approach to teaching the course.

Box 7.4: Ms. Marshall's Self-Reflection

I was worried about whether students would simply categorize one another. I found just the opposite to be true. In their papers, students were critical in analyzing both the "fit" and shortcomings of the model. What was also amazing to me was the students' ability to recognize differences in one another and respect those differences. By developing my own approach to discussing individual variations in a non-judgmental manner, I found that my initial anxiety shifted to confidence. The students followed my lead.

As the students study the Enneagram, they see things about one another that they didn't see before. As one student explained:

> I think being a Point 6 allows me to interact with Twos in many ways. I can see how Sixes and Twos balance each other in a way that is beneficial to both parties. This is because Sixes, or at least myself,

often like to be supportive and encouraging. Since Twos have a hard time putting themselves before others, a Six can encourage a Two to do so. A Six can at times have trouble making decisions. Twos can be enthusiastic and give the Six the support and enthusiasm to make decisions and feel confident in those decisions.

Another student observed:

In my family I am living with other Enneagram Threes: my mother and my sister. If we have a common objective in mind, things can go more smoothly than you imagine. But if we are at cross-purposes, putting all of our energies into opposing tasks, things can get pretty messy. I try to settle hotheaded people down, and often try to cool my own hotheadedness. I try to make them think practically, about how to solve problems efficiently. I don't appreciate griping about and lingering on problems. I help with tasks around my house, and believe that I am appreciated for it. Hard workers appreciate hard workers.

Ms. Marshall is overwhelmed by the interest and depth of insight of her students, as reflected in Box 7.5.

Box 7.5: Ms. Marshall's Self-Reflection
Their papers are astounding to me! I have learned how limited my earlier views were. I didn't appreciate the depth of objective understanding that students can develop about themselves at age 14 and 15. I'm so embarrassed that for years I have so underestimated my students.

One 14-year-old Point 6 writes:

After speaking to one of my dearest friends I now have five specific examples of how my Point 6 characteristics are beneficial to our friendship. First, my friend felt that in relationships I am insecure enough to need to keep checking on the status of our friendship, but secure enough to be an open, honest and loyal friend.

A Point 7 student writes:

It all adds to the suspense of life itself. Finding thrills and conquering obstacles against all odds is to me what makes life fulfilling. It is the feeling of knowing you beat something that many others would not be able to, a "rush." This gives me a sense of authority and pride. This is what propels me and motivates me.

By contrast, a quiet Point 5 shares:

There are many things that make me different from other people. On an Enneagram basis, I can completely detach and observe things from an outside point of view. As a matter of fact, I like being able to do that. When I understand something, like a biological process in science or the thought process of a really good friend, it isn't just a memorization of facts, I really understand it. I trust my own judgment most of the time, and I don't usually get affected by what is socially accepted. Material things don't matter to me, just as social status doesn't matter a whole lot.

Ms. Marshall feels greater respect for her students as she teaches the class, as reflected in Box 7.6.

Box 7.6: Ms. Marshall's Self-Reflection

I wish I could share all the papers with every teacher in the school. They are so instructive! Even more incredible are the conversations that go on between classmates as their eyes open to individual strengths that they never imagined before. I only wish I had learned to teach this course sooner. These students go so far beyond the insecurities of peer pressure we read about. Their curiosity about what makes people tick is aroused. Curious comments come back to me from other teachers and parents after talking with members of our class. Everyone is really interested in what we are doing.

Ms. Marshall's homework assignments encourage the students to talk with teachers, parents, and friends about the class. Ms. Marshall reports that a number of students have come to see her to learn more about the Enneagram after other students have mentioned it to them. Parents are also grateful to have a conversation with their teenagers about relevant views of the world. One parent reported the potential suicide of his child's friend, which had come to light in his child's discussion about the Enneagram and stress points. The parent came to the school counselor, who was able to intervene prior to a crisis. No one on the faculty had any idea there was a problem until the father had called.

Seeking Student Feedback

Surveys of Ms. Marshall's Enneagram classes over a four-year period allowed her to summarize what she learned from her students. While many students at first expressed confusion about the nature of this self-reflective process, they said they eventually learned a lot about themselves by studying the Enneagram. Below is a summary of these findings:

- Many students had previously judged themselves harshly be cause they exhibited certain natural personality traits (they are too shy or too different). They find it reassuring to learn that their personalities are simply a matter of normal wiring, and this self-acceptance often leads to greater tolerance of others.
- Some students find it hard to sit still for this type of difficult, introspective analysis. Many of them say that they do not like doing this type of work, but they admit they gain much from it.
- In general, students are more empathic and appreciative of each member of the class and feel that their common bond is strengthened. In addition, probably 50 percent of class members have reported discussing the class with parents at home as part of their assignments. This creates a wonderful basis for strengthening communication.

The self-reflection skills that students develop in Ms. Marshall's class can help them to make choices that support their inner emotional preferences. As with all tools that allow us to better understand ourselves, the Enneagram is only the beginning of a process. Ms. Marshall reports that after taking her class students are better able to reflect on themselves in a variety of situations.

Exhibit 7.1

The Enneagram Symbol:
Moving Toward or Away From Stressful Behavior

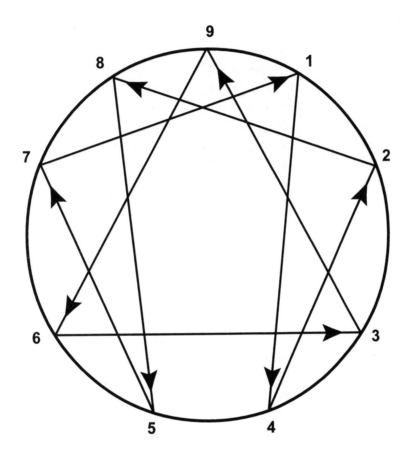

Each of the nine numbers around the edge of the circle represent the thematic story of an individual's pattern of behavior. The arrow that points <u>away</u> from number is the story of the individual's pattern of behavior under stress. The arrow that points <u>towards</u> the number is the story of the pattern of the individual's behavior when feeling secure.

Exhibit 7.2

The Enneagram Symbol: Moving Toward or Away From Stressful Behavior (Page 1 of 2)

Point #	Story	Famous Example
1	Realistic and holding high ideals, Ones have an inner sense of standards for "right" and "wrong". Teachers with a strong One have very high standards for how students will behave in their classroom. We see many social reformers identifying with this point.	Mahatma Gandi—a strong advocate for social reform in India through passive resistance.
2	Warm, sensitive and nurturing, Twos are focused on relationships and have an innate ability to sense what others need. Many Two teachers are able to understand the needs of children without words being necessary.	Princess Diana of England—known for her visits to the homes of sick children and needy people.
3	Energetic, confident and optimistic, Threes are focused on relationships and have an innate ability to sense what others need. Many Two teachers are able to understand the needs of children without words being necessary.	Jack Welsh, Chairman of General Electric—known for being a competitive task-master.
4	Sensitive and perceptive, Fours focus on developing new ways of seeing things or creating things that are different from the past. We often see many drama, art and music teachers who are Fours. They focus not on what is, but what is missing.	Robin Williams—an actor known for taking on unique roles that express a meaning or life purpose.
5	Introverted, analytical and insightful, Fives focus on detachment, observing and gaining information to test the integrity or dependability of the environment in which they live and work, whether it be a work system, a building or a concept.	Bill Gates, Chairman of Microsoft—a strategist who attends to big picture and details without getting in the public eye.

Exhibit 7.2 (continued)

The Enneagram Symbol:
Moving Toward or Away From Stressful Behavior (Page 2 of 2)

Point #	Story	Famous Example
6	Trusting and loyal, Sixes mentally question the safety and reliability of the world around them. Often demonstrating wit and intellect, sixes debate the merits of anything they are involved with and can procrastinate from coming to a final decision. Trust, relationships and alliances are important to them. They build communities.	Malcolm X, Civil Rights Leader—often misunderstood for his intellectual debate on the issue of race.
7	High energy, enthusiastic people who always have a lot of balls in the air. Seek variety, many options and ideas, adventure and a constant shift in venue. Many entrepreneurs seem to have a Seven focus, which gives them comfort in adapting to the constant evolution of the business.	Steven Spielberg, Movie Producer—his movies are a constant story of his adventures of interest.
8	Direct, self-assertive and self-reliant, Eights are often bosses who are interested in power and control. Comfortable with confrontation as a way of quickly getting information, they often have a strong instinctive sense of how to get things done. These are self-assertive people.	Martin Luther King, Civil Rights Leader—strong physical presence, symbol and leader who moved the movement into action.
9	Receptive and supportive, Nines have an instinctive ability "to walk in the shoes" of others. Able to "know" where everybody "is" on an issue, they are often strong negotiators, mediators and peacemakers.	Jimmy Carter, President—a strong mediator in many international disputes.

Exhibit 7.3

Enneagram Symbol Patterns of Stressed versus Secure Behavior

Possible Behavior when Stressed	Point	Possible Behavior when Relaxed
(-) 4: May turn anger inward and become depressed; look for what they don't have and become pessimistic; lose belief in themselves	1	(+) 7: Act more spontaneously and become less self-critical; relax and enjoy; become more flexible and optimistic
(-) 8: Become controlling and distrustful; become irritated easily and make demands; may isolate themselves	2	(+) 4: Become more self-expressive of creative side; accept painful feelings they may have and move on
(-) 9: Become indecisive and removed from themselves—working harder or numbing out with food or drugs; get disorganized and procrastinate	3	(+) 6: Get in touch with their feelings and connect with other people; see group rather than just their own values, needs and feelings
(-) 2: Deny their own needs and may get sick to get attention; may become dependent on others	4	(+) 1: Develop discipline and standards for putting their creativity to use; get positive, practical and committed to values; less sensitive
(-) 7: Become distracted, disorganized; may take on activities impulsively; withdraw into themselves	5	(+) 8: Get out of their heads and into their bodies; become assertive, more outspoken; take control and define limits
(-) 3: Stay too busy to avoid anxiety; resist trying new things to avoid failure; stay in perpetual state of indecision	6	(+) 6: Trust in themselves and their own judgement; see the big picture and put decisions in context; relax
(-) 1: Blame their problems on others; stay irritable; obsess on an idea or plan; become very critical	7	(+) 5: Become objective and explore themselves and their projects more in depth; recognize their fears and take themselves seriously
(-) 5: Withdraw from the action and may become depressed; become a little paranoid; may ignore their own feelings	8	(+) 2: Connect with others by revealing their softer, less controlling side; become better able to express warmth, affection and caring
(-) 6: Forget themselves by being too caught up in everyone else; immobilized by anxiety and worry; may be passive and lacking action	9	(+) 3: Gain confidence and optimism; get control over their lives and work; set direction and focus on what they want to do

8
Developing *Innersense*

The basic skills discussed in this chapter are designed to help adolescent students reflect on themselves and others in disciplined ways that progressively build their understanding of their own identities. It is extremely important that these tools be used in non-judgmental ways that encourage students to feel confident developing their self-awareness and comfortable with their resulting self-knowledge.

Adolescence is a major turning point for student self-awareness. Of the seven profound biological changes that occur during human life (including birth and death), three occur between ages of ten and fourteen (Sylwester, 1999): Growth of reproductive capabilities, maturation of the brain's structure to support social and ethical judgment, and development of personal and social identities. During adolescence, students need to adjust not only to physical changes in their bodies but also to sometimes overwhelming changes in emotional awareness.

We can help adolescents cultivate self-awareness as a means to interpret and understand their thoughts and feelings about themselves, which form the foundation of their emerging identity. We can encourage them to engage in a constructive and disciplined reflective process that will integrate their new thoughts and feelings into self-knowledge that reinforces their sense of purpose.

Box 8.1: Author Reflection (Claudia)

Adolescents' identity comes from information they process from the "inside-out" as well as the "outside-in." Unfortunately, in our media dense world, teenagers often receive a lot more "outside-in" information upon which to build their sense of peer identity. There are so many messages about what to wear, how to behave and how to compare oneself to others. I really believe we need to give adolescents equal information and a discipline to develop a deep way of thinking about themselves from the "inside out." If they can understand ways in which they are unique that add value to their peer relations, they gain confidence that can override more superficial comparisons.

Students have important emotional information available to them that can help them understand their thoughts and feelings in ways that are essential to answering questions about identity as well as peer relationships and external world influences.

Let's visit another classroom where Amanda Olsen shares her own experience as a middle-school counselor and health teacher introducing a disciplined approach to self-reflection to her seventh grade Human Growth and Development class. Box 8.3 describes her thoughts as she begins to teach reflective processes to her students.

Box 8.3: Mrs. Olsen's Self-Reflection

As I approach the task of introducing the reflective process to sixth to ninth graders, I feel a lot of anxiety because I understand that kids of this age do not really understand what self-reflection is. Self-reflection isn't reinforced in our culture. I also realize how difficult it is to teach and reflect at the same time. Certainly I was never taught self-reflection skills in school, so I sometimes feel that I am flying blind. But I also see the positive results in many adolescents who develop these skills. The importance of the task rallies me forward to somehow overcome the obstacles, and I gain confidence in my own sense of purpose.

As Mrs. Olsen begins, she explains to her students that sixth to ninth graders are going through a "majestic period" in their lives. The students may not know the meaning of the word "majestic," but Mrs. Olsen says it with so much passion that everyone in the room seems to straighten up and listen. She explains that this is the time when life gives them an opportunity to get in touch with the special qualities that will help them emerge into adulthood. She also refers to their "innersense" (Shelton, 1999), the self-reflecting that helps them develop a picture inside their minds of their unique personal qualities.

Mrs. Olsen further explains that, with help from a few basic skills, students will quickly understand the personal meaning of innersense. When the class discusses the topic further, one boy says, "I know exactly what you are talking about, I just never had a word for it. No one ever asked me about it before, so I assumed it wasn't important!" Mrs. Olsen describes innersense as a range of qualities that contribute to the formation of a self-concept: learning style, emotional awareness, communication style, natural decision-making style, values, intuition, and an emerging sense of life purpose, to name just a few. Recognizing the early signs of stress is especially important, and will be used as an anchor point for understanding whether an individual is vulnerable to a whole range of self-destructive behaviors including drinking, drugs, food abuse, bullying, and suicide.

The most important part of this exercise is not learning the precise definition of the terms, but the discovery process that students go through as they engage in self-reflection. They also begin to recognize that understanding each individual's innersense helps them learn how to complement the efforts of those around them.

Innersense Journal

Mrs. Olsen asks the students to keep a journal about their own innersense. She provides the students time in class to learn about different aspects of innersense, and then she asks them to write about their own views in their journal. She always asks them to record their individual thoughts in writing before the class discusses the topic. This way she can review individual points of view when she collects the journals each week, and write comments back to her students. Students have very different views about the strengths of their innersense.

One seventh grade girl writes, "By body language and tone of voice I can almost always tell that something is wrong with someone in my family. My mom says even when she thinks her private thoughts, I can sense what she is thinking."

A seventh grade boy states, "I am an introverted person, which shows in almost everything I do. I like to think about my answers in class before I express them. True to my character, I enjoy things that involve creativity. I find that in music, I can express the mood I am in at the time I create the piece."

By contrast, a more outgoing seventh grader explains, "I think that your innersense is clearly dependent upon your outer sense, and what people think of you. Because when push comes to shove, your innersense is what you don't want people to see. So your innersense is not what matters to others but only to yourself."

Mrs. Olsen further explains innersense to the students after they share their journal writing:

> In my experience as a teacher and counselor, I have found that students who don't learn to appreciate their innersense, or uniqueness as individuals, often feel ordinary, unimportant, and overlooked. The goal of this class is to help each of you understand what

makes you special, as you see it. It's not something I can tell you. In fact, in this class you will be the only one who can grade your work in terms of whether you have found the correct answer for you. I can only grade the data and documentation you show me to support the answer you have found.

Mrs. Olsen considers her students to be the experts at applying the models and frameworks that she presents; they determine for themselves whether a characteristic that the class explores is relevant to them. After all, they are the ones doing the original research. But Mrs. Olsen will grade them on the data and evidence they present about themselves to support their conclusions: for example, if a student believes she is "kind," she needs to be able to illustrate that trait in her writing with examples drawn from her real-life behavior.

Mrs. Olsen believes that trust is important in helping students to learn self-reflection. She honors the beliefs students hold about themselves—even when she does not necessarily think the perception is accurate. She knows that as students begin to document their beliefs with the information they gain in interviews with parents and friends, the students will have the opportunity to bring their beliefs about themselves into focus. The gradual learning process usually helps adolescents be less self-critical, as their data-gathering discussions help them learn about many positive characteristics others see in them. Mrs. Olsen ponders this question further through another self-talk, as described in Box 8.4.

Box 8.4: Mrs. Olsen's Self-Reflection

I feel mixed emotions about how I support my students. Many times it is really hard to hold back from making a judgment about the characteristics children see in themselves, particularly when my own observations suggest that the students are not being accurate. But I carefully allow the child to continue the self-reflective process without making a comment. I realize how vulnerable students feel during this process, and how one negative word can shut a student down. Allowing students to self-explore in a safe space takes a lot of discipline sometimes.

Helping Michael

Mrs. Olsen sees a relationship between a student's recognition and articulation of innersense and his or her motivation in school. The following is a great example of how a student's ability to articulate his innersense, combined with the reinforcement of his own picture by parents and teachers, led to significantly improved academic performance (Shelton, 1999, p. 62-63).

Michael was a seventh grader diagnosed with Attention Deficit Disorder. He was getting C's and D's in school. Mrs. Olsen administered to Michael the Murphy Meisgeir, a Myers-Briggs type indicator often used with younger students. In a one-on-one counseling session between Michael and Mrs. Olsen after she had administered the test, he was able to describe very clearly the qualities of his innersense. He used the Myers-Briggs framework as a starting point for articulating his self-identity.

> You know Mrs. Olsen, I really like action and adventure and taking risks. My dream is to own a sports shop in the country, and to have a lot of time to be with people who share my interests. Mountain biking is my first love. I don't need a lot of money—just a lot of time to bike and explore the country. I find academics so boring. I just can't keep my mind on class sometimes, even when I try hard.

Michael gave Mrs. Olsen a detailed plan about how he would accomplish his dreams. He also shared some of the anger and frustration he was feeling about how all anyone talked about to him was how badly he was doing in school. Mrs. Olsen was able to set up a conference with his parents to provide perspective. Here is what she told them:

> Michael is very clear about who he is and what he likes, and he is motivated toward his dream. He is charming and charismatic, and these qualities bring a great deal to life accomplishments. Unfortunately, he is frustrated with school, a quality that is not abnormal for many boys of his age. It's important that we view his academic achievements as one piece of his life, and not as the value of him as a person. Hopefully, this support will give Michael the freedom to bring his academics back into perspective.

As Michael's parents and other teachers began to see Michael's life from his perspective, they focused their discussions with him on things that he felt were important. Slowly, academics came into perspective as just one part of his life. Michael felt recognized by adults for who he was, and he began to release some of his anger. He also began to explore some tools that might help his attentiveness in the classroom. He stopped taking medication for ADD and slowly gained control over his classroom behavior through his own effort. By ninth grade, Michael was on the honor roll. More importantly, he felt valued for who he was.

How do kids like Michael develop the ability to be so insightful about their inner qualities? First, we as teachers have to make them and their interests an important focus of the educational process. Second, we have to help them build the self-reflective skills that enable them to see and appreciate themselves. Third, we should teach them to recognize basic skills, which help them to develop reflective abilities and strengthen their academic performance.

Exploring Temperament

Temperament is an innate emotional pattern of behavior that individuals demonstrate. Adolescents find the concept of temperament interesting to study, as they are totally focused on their personalities at this age. Mrs. Olsen reminds them that there is no "best" temperament; each has its pluses and minuses. The goal of understanding one's temperament is to understand the natural dimensions of our emotional wiring. There are a number of methods for defining and recognizing temperament; Mrs. Olsen uses the Myers-Briggs approach.

The Myers-Briggs Type Indicator (MBTI) is the most widely used psychological tool in the world. Professionals often use it in human resources, marriage counseling, career counseling, and other situations in which the understanding of individual differences is vital. Mrs. Olsen, however, uses the indicator both for its vocabulary and as a model for self-reflection. The essential point is not to arrive at a "correct" answer, but to explore a path that increases self-awareness. MBTI identifies four areas of natural preference that make up 16 different temperament types (see Exhibit 8.1). In Mrs. Olsen's class, students use MBTI to develop a vocabulary for examining their own personal preferences. They reflect on the results of the self-assessment technique and decide whether they seem to fit what they know of themselves. The students then write papers about their findings. For example, one boy wrote:

> I am a strongly introverted person, which shows in everything I do. Although I usually enjoy talking with one or two friends at school during lunch and break, I would rather spend time alone at home in my room than with another person. I also like to take my time to think about my answers before I express them. I am also a feeling person as opposed to a thinking person. When I make a decision pertaining to a person, I decide on the basis of how I feel about their cause, instead of what the facts are to support this. I will add the facts later.

Another student decided to point out the limitations of MBTI. "I think that a lot of times these 'tests' can be inaccurate depending on what type of mood the person taking them is in, or whether they are just naturally in between two preferences like Extroverted and Introverted." This is a perfectly appropriate answer, because our goal is to provide students with models for self-exploration that they are confident about.

A middle school history class used the COLORS system, which is based upon the Myers Briggs classification, to understand how each member of work groups uniquely approaches the decision making process involved in project collaboration. Different traits of the Myers Briggs System are represented as colors rather than names. Therefore, students were very interested in finding out whether they were "blue" or " orange" people, and how their individual pattern affected their ability to work in groups. When the teacher completed a unit of material, she assigned students to work on team projects. The students were amazed at how their color influenced, for example, attention to detail, and communicating with others, and impacted of group decision-making. This had great classroom results, in that the whole class realized that each group needed at least one "gold" person and one "blue" person to accomplish its goal!

Another use of temperament reflection is in studying the inner workings of historical figures. For example, in Mrs. McDonough's eighth grade history class, students use MBTI to compare and contrast the leadership styles of Thomas Jefferson and Andrew Jackson. The students collect data about each president from their reading and then debate which Myers-Briggs preference they believe each president represents. This helps them understand the inner dynamics that may have been behind the decisions of each president.

Mrs. McDonough observes that students develop conceptual skills to do this type of leadership analysis more effectively after learning the background for reflecting on personal style. Some students, who demonstrated weakness in this type of conceptual skill, perform strongly by utilizing the style model. Once they understand the idea of how you can reflect about the influence of temperament on leadership characteristics, they become more comfortable and skilled with this type of exercise without the use of the Myers Briggs.

Exhibit 8.1

The Four Myers-Briggs Preferences

1)   Source of Energy
     E/I:

     E preference people like to be with other people as a way to refresh their energy,
     while I preference people like to go off alone to refresh their energy. Both groups
     can be highly socially skilled

2)   How We Take In Information
     N/S:

     N preference people see the global picture first and the add the concrete details;
     S preference people like to see the concrete details first and then add the global
     picture

3)   Decision Making
     T/F:

     T preference people first apply logic and principle to making decisions, then
     consider values and circumstances; F preference people consider values and
     circumstances first and then apply logic and principles

4)   Natural Organization
     J/P:

     J preference people like to be organized and structured, and like making lists
     and using plan books—if they have free time, they will tend to organize it in
     advance; P preference people like to "go with the flow," resist lists and wait to the
     last minute to do things so they can incorporate their most recent thoughts—if
     they have free time, they will wait to see what emerges.

9
The Reality Check — Peer Feedback

Negotiating successfully through childhood and adolescence requires developing a realistic sense of who we are: what we can do or not do with ease; what has caused us to succeed or not to succeed academically or socially; and what we need to do to improve our performance in desired ways. To develop this evolving self-portrait, kids look to their own perceptions and listen to those of others. From the time they are very young, this interaction forms the basis of how they regard themselves. They listen to parents, teachers, and friends say, "you are terrific," or "what a great kid;" or they listen to those same trusted folks say "what a slob you are," or "can't you do anything right?" When kids hear something from the "outside," they unconsciously contrast it against what they think of themselves on the "inside."

Chapter 9 provides a skill-building process to help students effectively gather "outside" information and objectively listen to it in comparison to their "inside" information. Giving and receiving peer feedback effectively is a very important skill for students to develop to manage relations with peers and social groups. As exhibit 9.1 shows (at the end of this chapter), the process of "me knowing about me" is derived both from the inside and from the outside. The "me about me" is self-reflection: we focus our attention inward to gather emotional information, thoughts and impressions, and hear our own self-talk. Essential to development of self-awareness skills is complementary skill building in the "you about me": the process of giving and receiving objective feedback from others, especially peers. From the early years it is the constant interchange between inner reflection and outer feedback that develops a healthy and realistic sense of self that is so important to adolescent passage.

Skill in giving and receiving feedback can be developed from kindergarten through 12th grade as students become increasingly perceptive and articulate. The ability to be objective and non-judgmental as both a giver and receiver of feedback is essential. Effective listening and concrete observation skills are also important. Welcoming both positive and negative feedback is a skill difficult for many adults. It takes discipline and constant practice to impart these skills to our students. In Chapter 9 we will observe how the giving and receiving of feedback can be developed at four stages of learning: grades two, five, seven and nine.

Box 9.1: Author Reflection (Claudia)

When I work with students, particularly as they approach adolescence, I find that those who are looked up to by both teachers and other students are those who are particularly skilled in the *mediation* of perceptions between an inner sense of self and outer feedback from others. They do not try to force their views on others, or try to gain popularity by acting like whoever they think are "the popular kids." Instead, they have an inner sense of who they are, and constantly scan their environment to understand the views of others around them—bringing the two views simultaneously into focus. The resulting reality check helps them to keep both their sense of self and their relationship with others fresh, responsive and up to the moment.

Second Graders Begin the Feedback Process

Mr. Lomango teaches his second graders about how to give feedback through lessons combining English and art classes. The art teacher has each of the students lie down on large size brown packing paper, where he traces the outline of the student's body with a large magic marker. Each student spends the rest of the period drawing face, clothes and personal identifiers.

In English class, Mr. Lomango introduces a list of words that can be used to describe people. He chooses a number of adjectives, which students practice defining and spelling. After Mr. Lomango hangs their self-portraits on the walls around the classroom, he has each student pick a name out of a hat of one of their classmates. (Of course, you can't pick your own name.) Each student then writes three words on the portrait of the person whose name was picked—the words describing how the person contributes in class.

The students take the exercise very seriously, and pick very positive words. On the following days in English class, Mr. Lomango starts the period by picking two of the brown paper portraits and asks the class to talk about the ways in which each of these students contribute to the class. Afterward, each portrait student must thank the class for the feedback and make any self-observations about what he or she learned from the discussion. For example, Freddie says, "I was surprised you think I am quiet because my mom says I never stop talking."

Within two weeks, each child thus has a chance to be the subject of the feedback discussion. Mr. Lomango has generally positive feelings about the exercise:

Box 9.2: Mr. Lomango's Reflection

This exercise takes a lot of focus from me, but it is worth it. In order to keep the students interested, I have to be prepared to keep asking questions and probing information about each student. I have to keep the class moving quickly to hold interest. I have to keep the discipline structured so students learn to take each step seriously. However, the result can influence the climate of the class. Students become more open to one another. There is less fighting on the playground. Students who are tough on themselves are always surprised by how many good things their classmates can say about them. The whole environment becomes less stressful for all of us. It also provides wonderful feedback for parents in conferences. And when I find a child has real difficulty with the exercise, I am alerted to watch more closely for other signs of anxiety.

Fifth Grade Interviews

By fifth grade, the peer feedback exercise can utilize the expanded vocabulary and social interaction skills of the students. Ms. Mendoza introduces a unit in her English class, which she calls "Detective Work." Before the class she identifies a list of pairs of students, who are each assigned to gather feedback about ways the other contributes to the class. Each class member knows that he or she will be both the observer and the subject of observation, which keeps the feedback positive.

The class breaks into groups of three people, with none of the feedback-paired students working together. Each student asks the other members of his group about how his assigned student contributes to the class, and then summarizes this information in several paragraphs handed into Ms. Mendoza at the end of class. Ms. Mendoza reviews the written description and writes back several comments and questions, which the student will need to answer to complete his essay about his assigned student. Ms. Mendoza reviews the final essays before students meet in their assigned pairs to present their essays and comments to one another. Ms. Mendoza finds the whole process to be both interesting and worthwhile.

Box 9.3: Ms. Mendoza's Reflection

I find I learn a lot about how my students see each other and the class during this exercise. It is exciting to me to have the opportunity to ask questions that make students think more deeply about one another, as well as what makes the class beneficial for all of us. It is also magical for those students who believe no one ever notices them to realize just how noticed they really are. Seeking to learn more about another student forces each of them to learn more about themselves and their class dynamics. Once the students practice this model several times in closely monitored steps, I find they can transfer it with ease to their other classes.

Reflective Feedback for Seventh Graders

The objective of Mrs. Olsen's seventh grade "Reflective Feedback" unit is to help students explore their thoughts and feelings about themselves and one another and articulate their conclusions to others. They need practice expressing their awareness of themselves and others, including classmates and their teacher, in ways that are nonjudgmental yet concrete. This unit, which is part of Mrs. Olsen's Human Growth and Development class, is coordinated with the English and history curricula, so that the self-reflection process taught by Mrs. Olsen can be used by students to process feedback on English and history projects.

Mrs. Olsen also uses this process to help her students target where they want their contributions to be recognized in the classroom.

Box 9.4: Mrs. Olsen's Reflection

Teachers have a way of continually rewarding those extroverted children who speak up often in class; however, this may not acknowledge the more subtle contributions of introverted children who prefer to contribute in writing or in smaller group discussions. I want to make sure I differentiate my learning strategies so that I reach children who are comfortable contributing in a variety of ways, and then help them to broaden their opportunities to other spheres of the classroom.

As a part of the *self-feedback* process, students are asked in the beginning of the term to identify where they will make their primary contributions to the class: in large-group, full-class discussions; small-group discussions with peers; one-on-one discussions with other members of the class; or written comments in a weekly journal. They write down their personal objectives in a contract, which they give to Mrs. Olsen, and review their progress with her about every four to six weeks. In this way, mutual expectations are clear between teacher and student, and both introverted and extroverted children can have their contributions valued in a manner of choice. Periodically, objectives can be adjusted by student or teachers.

Peer feedback is also processed in Mrs.Olsen's class, where she assigns five students as "student peer reviewers" to provide feedback about class contributions to each student in the class. Mrs. Olsen instructs the class before this process begins:

> This is an exercise that can be difficult for seventh graders, but I believe this class is capable enough to do it. I want you to give feedback to your classmates in a way that you would want to receive it. Discuss both your positive and negative comments in ways that you would want to hear them. I will be reviewing the comments before you return them to the student. The student will also be giving me feedback on the usefulness of your feedback.

Mrs. Olsen has the class agree to four or five criteria in advance that the students will use to provide one another with verbal and written feedback. Mrs. Olsen assigns a grade on the feedback provided to the student based on the depth of discussion and the facts gathered to support the peer reviewer's points. The student being reviewed also provides comments to Mrs. Olsen after receiving his feedback, about how useful the comments were and how he plans to use them to modify any classroom behaviors.

Finally, Mrs. Olsen believes it is important to receive feedback about her own classroom contributions at least once a semester. She asks her students to identify in writing the three best contributions she makes to the class, and the three things she does that they would like to see her modify. Students are usually honest in their reactions and will provide useful comments. Mrs. Olsen looks forward to the feedback from students, as reflected in Box 9.5.

Box 9.5: Mrs. Olsen's Self-Reflection

I really feel excited about the opportunity to get feedback from students. When I first did this exercise, I let the students do it confidentially. Yet after doing self-feedback and peer feedback, I found the students developed the confidence and trust to tell me what they thought. Knowing that a student can give both positive and negative comments without feeling fear is a great reward. I truly feel blessed to really get to know these kids. Part of the trust I build with them requires a lot of discipline on my part—not to allow myself to rise to judgment. I have to practice staying in the safe harbor of self-awareness during every class.

Ninth Graders Explore Peer Identity Strategies

During adolescence, the whole subject of peer feedback becomes extremely important to students, as they are forming a whole picture in their minds of who they are. The classroom can be an important place for high school students to assess how they define themselves in connection to other people including friends, family, community, workgroup and the world at large. Let's consider a practical example of how this personal assessment can take place in the classroom.

In health class, Ms. Marshall asks her ninth grade students to consider the following reflection-provoking question:

> I'd like you to imagine a line measuring from left to right from zero to one hundred percent. Put an "X" at the point that demonstrates how much of your personal identity is influenced by your own independent thoughts, as opposed to the influence of other people e.g. friends, family, media, etc. So, for example, if you put your "X" at 42, that means you believe 42 % of your identity is influenced by you alone and 58% by others. There is no right or wrong answer to this. After you record you opinion in your journal, we'll talk about it together.

The students are intrigued by the question. Clearly it captures their attention, and they think about their answers for some time before finally writing their comments in their journals. After an interesting debate about the "best" place to put your mark, the students come to a consensus with the help of Ms. Marshall that there is no "right" or "wrong" place to put the mark. There are trade-offs, however. Students who see their identity influenced largely by others are more vulnerable to the influences of the crowd. Yet without consideration of peer opinions, students may be isolated from others.

Ms. Marshall is surprised by her own reactions to the students' discussion.

Box 9.6: Ms. Marshall's Reflection

I always thought it was "best" to have my identity formed primarily by my own thinking but I realize now how socially isolated some of the students, who took that position, feel from the class. Having the chance to debate this issue through the fresh and honest perspectives of my students helped me to reconsider the question for myself.

This exercise helped this middle school class consider the inside-out/outside-in perception mediation process in a way that they can understand and ponder. The use of the self-feedback, peer feedback and teacher feedback processes introduced in Mrs. Olsen's class become even more important for students as they enter high school.

Positive Identity Building on a Weekend Away

A weekend retreat for a diverse group of urban middle school girls was organized by the Double Discovery Center at Columbia University, in New York City. The event focused on building leadership skills for these young girls, many of whom had never been out of their "hood" before; never encouraged to dream; never taught about how to work with themselves and their strengths to get ahead in the world. Many of these girls were reflecting for the first time about who they were, what they wanted for themselves, and how to get there.

Box 9.7: Author Reflection (Robin)

As one of the facilitators for this weekend, I am reminded of how important positive peer feedback is, and how little time we spend as educators really encouraging others to engage in it. Descriptive words, when spoken and written, are so powerful to these girls. I remember in my junior high years, peer regard was so important – especially for those kids who felt on the outside…but, important in some way to all of us. I have the feeling that this experience will be defining for many of these participants. I know this weekend is not enough and I hope to have more time with these girls reinforcing and identifying their strengths and helping them to confront their challenges.

As part of the theme of having girls get getting to know themselves of the weekend, facilitators asked each girl to find and work with a partner, taking turns lying down on the floor on drawing paper while the partner outlined the body of the other. This part of the exercise was the "you about me" part, making obvious the point that we form our self perception from the inside and from the outside too. The act of drawing and of lying down on the paper was the fun and giggles part!! Then, in a more serious moment, each girl had to write three descriptive words about her partner, on the figure she had just drawn. This was intriguing and challenging for most. They spent time thinking about the words they would use. We asked the girls to be positive and to stay away from physical attributes. Here are a few examples of the words used: One participant said of her partner " shining, fun-loving, spiritual;" another's drawing included the words " warm, friendly, generous". After writing the words on the partner's silhouette, each team presented the drawing first to her partner and to the group as a whole. The girls really liked this part of the program (after they got past the "sorry that I have no artistic talent" part). It was an opportunity to listen to a public presentation of positive aspects of themselves. It was a first-time experience for many.

This proved to be a powerful exercise for the girls. Some, used to only criticism and teasing, had never gotten positive feedback before. Some were embarrassed by it, and said later that they secretly felt good about it. Others openly welcomed the positive words and wanted more! In any case, these girls now had new personal data to include in their self-perceptions.

The next part of the exercise (the "me about me" part) took place as each girl filled out in her own silhouette drawing with words or pictures. Facilitators created times in the weekend schedule for the girls to stop and reflect on themselves and to add to their picture. The social-emotional results were terrific. The participants used the silhouettes as a record keeper for themselves, and took the opportunity to be more reflective and thoughtful. They talked about taking the drawing home to remind them of the weekend and of the positive feedback they had received.

Exhibit 9.1

Reflective Sources of Identity

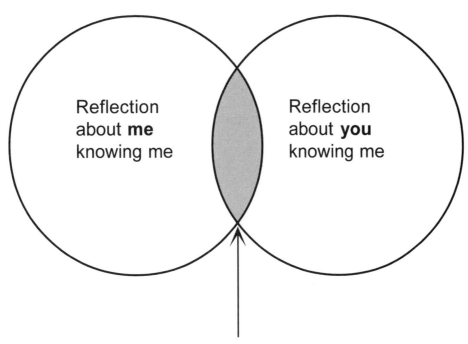

Reflection about **me** knowing me

Reflection about **you** knowing me

Personal identity emerges from the constant giving and receiving of information from self and others. Objective skills in giving and receiving peer feedback can help this process to be effective for the adolescent.

10
Emotional Technologies

Speaking at a conference on digital technology and social-emotional learning at Columbia University in 1999, James Comer remarked that at the beginning of the new millennium, for the first time in history, most of the information our children receive about the world beyond their own households is not filtered through the adults who are responsible for their care and education (Comer, J., 1999). Let's think for a moment about what he meant by that startling statement.

Families and communities have traditionally transmitted one generation's knowledge, attitudes, and values to the next quite directly, either personally or through community institutions, with (for better or for worse) relatively little interference from outside influences. But successive waves of communications technologies—from photography and telegraphy to the advent of film, television, and computers—have brought us into the Digital Age. These days in industrialized nations, including the United States, we are all increasingly "connected" to the world beyond our own communities through cell phones, televisions, Internet, and a myriad of other technological marvels. Our students spend hours, usually unsupervised by an adult, listening to radio or watching television, working on computers and accessing the Internet, and playing computer or video games.

As educators and parents, we are responsible for teaching our children how to use these technologies wisely. Self-awareness and social-emotional skills are among the tools we can provide to help children cope with the flood of images and information they are exposed to through the mass media—much of which is commercially driven, involving both direct and subliminal appeals to the emotions of the reader/listener/viewer, and may or may not represent the ideas and values we wish to foster.

In this chapter and the next, we will focus on the intersection between the promotion of self-awareness and social-emotional learning (SEL), and two very different applications of technology: computer programs designed by educators, and television commercials produced by the advertising industry (Chapter 11). We strongly believe that these media will earn their place in the classroom, and will serve teachers in differentiating the classroom and students in facilitating their unique styles of learning.

Taking Advantage of Computer Technology

Each day millions of kids log on to computers in their homes or schools or even at a nearby library to work on school assignments, play interactive games, e-mail their friends, or explore the Internet. Although young people usually choose to use these technologies for entertainment and personal communication, educators and curriculum developers understand the power of this technology as a tool for learning. You can access encyclopedias, dictionaries, and reference books of all kinds via the Internet—or buy them on CD-ROM—and math, science, history, and language arts software programs are available both for schools and for direct sale to the public. Interactive computer programs also offer great promise for teaching skills in the realm of social and emotional development.

The example we've chosen for discussion here is *Relate for Teens*, a software program created by Ripple Effects, Inc., which is designed to help adolescents deal constructively with some of the social-emotional challenges they encounter in their everyday lives. We selected this particular software tool to share with you because as far as we know it's the most comprehensive digital tool for social-emotional learning available at this time, and is well-suited for classroom use. I (Robin) have personally worked with *Relate for Teens* at home with my own children and in several studies at The Institute for Learning Technologies at Teachers College, Columbia University, where I teach a course in Emotional Intelligence and Digital Technology. In both contexts the software got high marks for interest level, engagement, and the potential of real education and skill training in social-emotional skills.

Classroom differentiation strategies are supported easily by the software, as teachers can effectively group students with similar learning needs and styles with a particular computer exercise, and tailor the content exercise to student learning needs.

Engaging Kids with *Relate for Teens*

The *Relate for Teens* software provides a fun educational experience, free of time and place restrictions, with privacy and tolerance built into the experience itself. From a design perspective, it is eye-catching and age specific. Visual and audio components reflect the trends and fashions of today's youth: cell phones, baggy jeans, and graffiti are among the elements used to achieve a feeling of relevance and reality (see Exhibit 10.1, at the end of this chapter).

The power of *Relate for Teens* lies in its embracing multiple modes of learning: straightforward information, real-life examples of issues of interest to adolescents, basic skills training in social and emotional competencies, self-assessments, and journaling. The program provides students with a multimedia "learning laboratory" on the computer, one that they can use to explore and practice self-awareness and emotional skill-building. Students can use this software either in collaboration with others or privately at their own pace, and the program can be integrated into a larger classroom curriculum.

Relate for Teens walks users through a vast array of contemporary problems typically faced by adolescents (see Exhibit 10.2, at the end of this chapter). Some of the issues presented, such as nail-biting, are relatively simple and superficial; others, like drug and alcohol abuse and AIDS awareness, are more serious and more complex. Users can approach each subject through a number of possible "game" options. For example, they can watch video clips of other teenagers from a range of ethnic backgrounds struggling with a problem; they can choose to learn more about a specific topic, including suggestions on how to resolve a problem presented; and they can also obtain contact information for additional sources of guidance and support.

One eighth-grade student named Josh says, "I think the program is very helpful. It's a good way to get advice on a topic if you don't want someone to know about it or to butt into your life."

Another attractive feature of *Relate for Teens* is an electronic journal, which is included to provide a forum for each student to jot down his or her observations, thoughts, and feelings on issues raised in the program's modules (see Exhibit10.3, at the end of this chapter). The journal also serves as a space for self-reflection. The journal is private and accessible only by a pass code. Josh thinks students enjoy using this software because it engages them and it's all about them. Emily, another seventh-grader, says the software is "really cool because there are always questions that help you think about yourself."

For two years, New York City's School of the Future, a middle school in lower Manhattan, participated in a pilot program to test the viability of teaching empathy with a computer program as an integral teaching tool in the whole curriculum package. Like many urban public schools, the NYC School of the Future is home to a diverse student population, and, as might be surmised from its name, it is also technology oriented, with a computer-savvy student body. Graduate students from

Teachers College, Columbia University, and New York University joined guidance counselor Jonathon Gray to support seventh-grade humanities teacher Melissa Moskowitz in teaching this program.

Using SEL Software in the Classroom

Melissa Moskowitz, a teacher extremely popular with her students, was eager to try *Relate for Teens* in her classroom. She easily incorporated use of the software twice a week into her regular curriculum. Between her enthusiasm and her students' willingness to interact with new technologies, the climate for the program was optimal. In her opinion, *Relate for Teens* proved to be a good tool to get students thinking about their feelings and their reactions to the kinds of situations they face in real life, and in the classroom.

While the program includes "scope and sequence" possibilities to guide teachers to use the software, it's flexible enough that teachers need not follow a predetermined sequence to use it in their classrooms. Instead, they can adapt the software to fit their own teaching styles as well as the learning styles and individual needs of their students. While students will naturally be drawn in by the game aspect of the program, it is still important for teachers to follow a lesson plan integrating Relate into their curriculum, as it is not a "stand-alone", but rather a set of activities that need to be strategically integrated, with both teacher and students interacting and invested in the potential benefits of "the game."

As we join Ms. Moskowitz in her classroom, she's working with a customized "scope and sequence" that has been designed to build an understanding of what empathy is, and to foster development of that key social-emotional capacity. This is part of the software's empathy module, which encourages students to view problems from multiple perspectives, examining their own behaviors and attitudes. Before she begins this session with her class, Ms. Moskowitz takes a moment to pay attention to her own thoughts and feelings, as described in Box10.1.

Box 10.1: Ms. Moskowitz's Self-Reflection

I'm thinking about how perfect this is for my students. They're kids who really like to be on the computer. But I do have reservations about whether or not the kids will take learning social and emotional skills on a computer seriously instead of just treating it like a game. I'm sure I am not alone in this concern, but I like new things and new approaches, which the computer has such potential of providing. If it works, then I would be excited about the potential of using this tool to get down a lot of objective material about students. I know that I could benefit from some of these exercises myself!

Ms. Moskowitz turns her attention back to the class and organizes students in pairs in front of the classroom computers. She explains the project to them and tries to start a class discussion by asking students to think about the observable behaviors that foster empathy. The students look interested, but they don't have much to say. They seem more eager to start working on their computers, so Ms. Moskowitz tells them to begin by focusing on "listening," one of the "skills and concepts" that the program identifies as behavioral components of empathy (others are "respect," "kindness," and "courtesy").

The students are soon immersed in exploring what the program has to offer relating to the topic at hand. As one pair watches a Relate video clip of someone talking about what it means to listen, one of them remarks, "This is cool. These are real kids here." A little later another student call out, "Hey, Ms. Moskowitz! This is what *you* teach us about how to listen. Cool." Ms. Moskowitz encourages the students to take careful look at the "how to" section on listening and to reflect on their own listening skills. After they've worked in their pairs for a while, she picks one of the open-ended questions included in the software to put to the class as a whole. In this case, the text on the screen asks the students to imagine how they would feel if someone wasn't listening to them. She now finds them ready, eager to talk—and to listen—and the discussion takes off.

Relate for Teens includes hundreds of topics for students to explore on their own, as well in pairs or small groups, during class time set aside for that purpose, or during "free" or study hall periods. Think of anything that bothered you, concerned you, or had a major impact on your life during your middle and high school years, and it will most likely be included as a topic in the program. With privacy just a mouse-click away (the software includes a feature that hides the contents of the screen with the click of an icon), students can take a personality profile, assess their understanding of a particular topic, explore difficult subjects, and practice skill-building at their own pace.

This is all possible through a feature that allows each student to set up an individual "account" when they first enter the program. This creates a sense of ownership, as well as the opportunity to have one's own separate dialogue with the program in a way comfortable to the user. (A teacher from one of the other classes trying out the *Relate for Teens* software commented that it was an especially good tool for shy students, who can use the game to explore feelings that they would be reluctant to share in a group setting.)

For her part, Ms. Moskowitz is pleased when she reflects on her students' work with *Relate for Teens.*

Box 10.2: Ms. Moskowitz's Self-Reflection

This program is good! I like it. I like what I see in my students. I want to make sure that I am going to be able to use this program to get more information about them, to help them use the software to train where they most need it, and skip the sections they seem to have down pat. I am not sure why some were less enthused. Most kids, like I thought they would, really got into it. I wonder if they gave their true answers. I really like that the software has an educational bent. I enjoy it myself. I can look up anything that troubles me and there it is!! I find myself eager to see the results of the assessments and to listen to the true life videos. Much potential here. I only hope I can realize it by being very upbeat, by including it effectively and by modeling. I feel good and positive about this and I hope it comes across.

Ms. Moskowitz sees the potential of using the software as an effective tool for teaching. The results of the pilot study were very promising. Students learned a great deal about empathy and its components, and increased their empathic behavior in the classroom. Ms. Moskowitz suggestions for next time included more class time for the program, role-playing, and practice opportunities.

Teachers who plan to use the program need to take time to familiarize themselves with it, map out strategies for integrating it organically into curriculum, and create an environment supportive of individualized learning. Students need to feel free to explore the program, to complete assessments on their own, and to write in their private journals without fear of judgment. Allowing students to use the software throughout the day, as well as during scheduled class time, can increase student ownership and control over their own progress.

The social-emotional learning at the heart of Relate for Teens—and similar programs available now or in development—thus becomes an ongoing development of life skills, rather than just another topic. When integrated with other parts of the curriculum, such programs hold great promise for helping children learn skills to negotiate their lives more effectively, more compassionately, and more fully. For teachers, the digital age brings additional "hands" to the classroom for understanding different styles of learning and accommodating individualized instruction.

Box 10.3: Author Reflection (Robin)

Since my visit to the classroom, Ripple Effects has come out with another, more sophisticated program for teens to celebrate diversity and build resilience, to educate about trauma and coping with troubled times. I just received a copy myself and really like it! *Relate* is wonderful – for education, for peeking in on what others are thinking, for exploring. I appreciate the power of this resource and only wish its use could be more widespread. I believe that students can become more and more comfortable with learning about themselves in this way. I look forward to the opportunity to do more research and to integrating the software with real time practice.

Exhibit 10.1

Relate for Teens

Exhibit 10.2

Relate for Teens Challenge

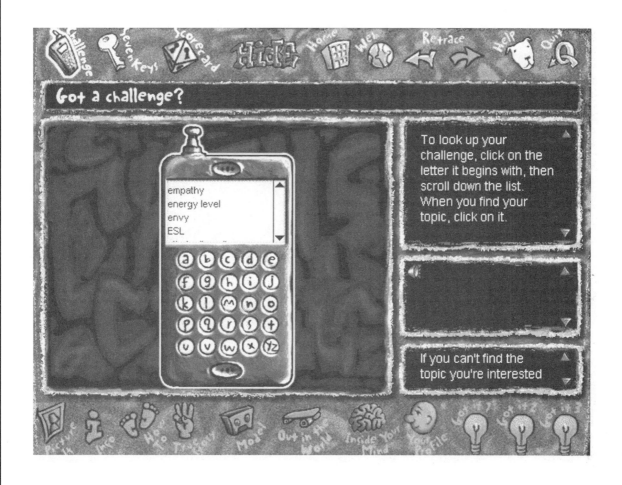

Exhibit 10.3

Relate for Teens Journal

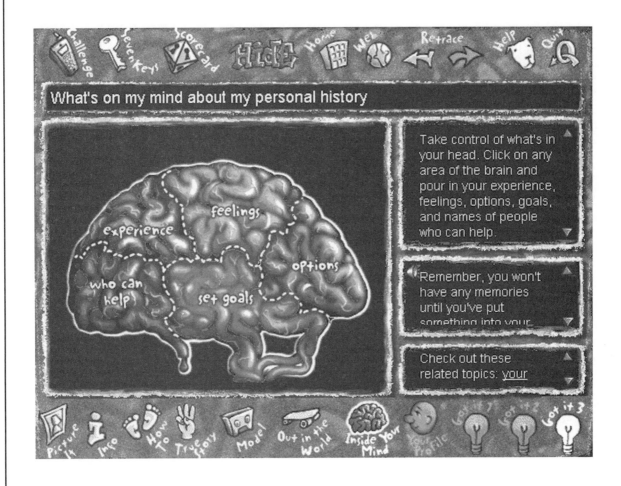

11
Media Lessons

According to an article in the Journal of the American Academy of Child and Adolescent Psychiatry, the average family watches twenty-one hours of television a week (Villani, 2000). Other researchers report that 32 percent of young children between ages two and seven have televisions in their rooms, as do 65 percent of preteens and adolescents age eight to eighteen (Roberts et all, 1999).

Leaving aside for the moment the question of the content of the TV programs themselves, commercials are an inevitable aspect of television programming and can have a significant impact on children. One estimate puts the number of TV ads children see per year at 40,000 as of 2001 (Kunkel, 2002). Advertisers have done a great deal of research to determine what appeals to different demographic groups including younger children, "tweens," and adolescents. The techniques they use to target these "market segments" have become increasingly sophisticated. These commercials communicate strong messages, evoking a range of reactions, thoughts, and emotions about what is valued in today's society.

Analyzing Commercials to Raise Emotional Awareness

In this chapter we take a brief look at a ten-session course developed by Robin Stern and two Columbia University, Teacher's College graduate students, Shetal Shah and David Walcyk, with consultation from classroom teacher Linsay Obrig. It is targeted to help fourth- and fifth-graders analyze and critique commercials to learn more about themselves, and to help them better interpret the advertising to which they are exposed. Television commercials offer an opportunity to develop self-awareness and critical thinking skills. They may also be used to help children understand both the differences between their feelings, thoughts, and actions; and the differences between their own thoughts and feelings and what someone else wants them to think and feel.

Box 11.1: Author Reflection (Robin)

As many of my international college students at Columbia University point out, America is way behind the proverbial "8 ball" in using media as a teaching tool for critical thinking. TVs are on all over America much of the time, and offer an easy way to get the attention of kids. I believe TV programming and commercials provide a terrific opportunity for teachable moments in the classroom. I am pleased to have a chance to showcase the work of these students and of Trevor Day School in the area of media literacy. Co-teaching this lesson will require awareness on the part of all facilitators.

Getting Kids to Think About Feelings

Language arts teacher Lindsay Obrig is teaching this course during mini-term at Trevor Day Middle School in New York City. Mini-term allows students to take elective courses in between their academic semesters. Along with Lindsay, co-author Robin and Columbia University Teacher's College graduate students Shetal Shah and David Walczyk developed and delivered this course to 10 students. Ms. Obrig and Dr. Stern were constants in the classroom during the mini-term session as coach and observer, with Shetal and David present to co-teach several sessions each.

The goal of the course's first exercise is to help students understand the difference between their thoughts and feelings. What they think about a commercial may be very different from how they feel about it. Children need to be able to differentiate between the two.

Before Ms. Obrig begins the class she pauses for a moment to reflect in Box 11.1.

Box 11.1: Ms. Obrig's Self-Reflection

I'm very eager to begin this "Watching TV" course. I love film and television, and I'm really excited about the possibility it holds for education. I'm so curious to see how children will react. I really want to be able to help kids be more aware of how TV affects their emotional life, and how their critical awareness can help them make better decisions.

Ms. Obrig begins by asking students to close their eyes and try to remember what they were feeling and thinking when they first woke up in the morning. The students talk about feeling tired. The class discusses the differences between the physical sensation of being tired or cold, and emotions like anger or sadness. The students seem to understand this distinction.

Next Ms. Obrig asks the students to close their eyes and focus on their present emotions. She asks them to think about how they would like to feel at the end of the day, and then to think about something they could do to help get them there. The goal is to help the kids understand that they themselves can influence the course of the day just by being more aware of themselves, their options, and their goals, and by taking action on their own behalf rather than simply reacting.

A girl named Chelsea says, "Well, right now I'm still a little annoyed at my brother because he changed the television channel I was watching. But I wish I could feel happy by the end of the day, so maybe I can talk to myself about how he didn't do it to torture me and he is really nice most of the time."

Ms. Obrig knows that taking part in the sharing exercise herself often helps her students begin the reflective process and feel more open to participating, so she shares some of her own morning thoughts with the class: "I woke up this morning feeling a little worried about everything I had to do this week at school. I knew that I promised to give back your papers by tomorrow, and I worried about finding the time to finish reading them all. So I said to myself, 'OK, there's a lot to do, and I better use my plan book to organize myself.' Boy, did I feel better."

This kind of sharing on the part of a teacher, about appropriate topics and within commonsense limits, is helpful to students. It gives them an example of what proponents of social-emotional learning call positive self-talk, which we discussed in Chapter 1, and an illustration of how to use self-talk to gain mastery over their feelings.

Watching the Commercials

Next, Ms. Obrig leads a brief discussion about commercials in general: their purpose, their goals, and how they achieve those goals. The students learn that commercials often attempt to evoke a feeling in viewers by telling a story. Then their teacher asks the class to watch three commercials she has taped for them. She also asks them to record on their class worksheets what the story is for each commercial, what feelings the story evokes, and how effectively the creators convey their story and its intended emotions (see Exhibit 11.1, at the end of this chapter).

Prior to the class, a selection of three commercials were videotaped from TV shows that students of this age watch. The commercials are described in the following section, together with student reactions.

Commercial 1: Barbie as Mother

This commercial is filmed with lots of bright pink and other "pretty" colors. It opens with three happy babies sitting on a cloud. Next comes a few shots of a Barbie doll as a mother with her Barbie-like baby, shown in a range of motherly activities. The scene then changes to a real girl, holding her doll and pretending that Barbie is a mother. The girl looks very happy.

The students discuss their reactions to the commercial. (Not surprisingly, the girls take the lead since this is about Barbie.) Melissa says, "I know why they show real babies at the beginning of the commercial. It makes you feel like a real mommy."

Another student, Katie, says, "The colors and the music make me feel happy, even though I don't play with Barbie anymore. Maybe they wanted you to feel like a mom rocking your baby."

Jasmine adds a note of pure skepticism, "I think the whole thing is too fake. It's like you have to look perfect to be a real mom."

A lively five-minute debate ensues. Then Ms. Obrig tells the class it's time to look at the next ad.

Commercial 2: Michael Jordan Sneakers

The next commercial flashes a series of quick, seemingly unconnected images on the screen, including a bathtub overflowing with water and a shot of children running around. We hear loud music. The final scene shows Michael Jordan sinking a basketball shot. This time when Ms. Obrig opens the discussion both boys and girls jump in.

One boy says, " I don't like this commercial. I thought it was confusing."

This contrasts sharply with other reactions. "I thought the commercial was awesome," a boy named Brian says. "I felt really excited while I was watching it. They're trying to tell you the story that if you buy those sneakers you can play basketball like Michael Jordan. I would buy the sneakers!"

Hannah says, "I didn't know what it was about. I felt confused, and I didn't like it until the end. Then I felt happy that the guy got the basket. I didn't think anything about sneakers, though."

"Hold those thoughts," Ms. Obrig says, and then she shows the third commercial.

Commercial 3: Public Service Announcement about AIDS

This commercial opens with background choral music. A series of bold words flash up on the screen: "fear," "love," "hope," and "stress." A child is shown sitting alone in a large open space. A series of images of city life appear on the screen, followed by a message that informs the viewer that pregnant women with AIDS can prevent their babies from being infected with the disease. The commercial is very sobering and the class reacts somberly.

"I felt so sad," says Kate. "I wish we didn't have to see that. I felt upset for the babies and sad that some people still get sick with AIDS. I think they wanted us to feel sad."

Miranda says, "I felt sad, but I felt hopeful too, because I thought if you can find out early you can save the baby from getting AIDS."

As the discussion continues, it's clear that the students understand that television commercials are designed to appeal to emotion in order to persuade, most often to sell a product. But the students seem to lack the ability to take this knowledge to the next level—that is, to consider what affect television advertising has on their everyday lives.

Still, they've accomplished a lot on this first day. Ms. Obrig ends the session by assigning homework: each student is asked to watch three commercials and fill out an evaluation sheet on each. The next two sessions are devoted to sharing and discussing the results in class.

At the end of the first week, Ms. Obrig considers her own thoughts about how the course is going (Box 11.2).

Box 11.2: Ms. Obrig's Self-Reflection

I am happy with the way this class has gone. I'm pleased that the students were easily able to move into the mode of self-reflection. As we continue, students are becoming more nuanced in their description of their feelings. Their vocabularies are expanding, and their reflective abilities are improving. Next time I teach this course, I will be able to move them forward more quickly. It is so interesting to see and hear the difference in individual responses— what each child focuses on and builds upon in his own commercial. Their differing perception of story lines will be helpful information down the road.

Taking the Perspective of the Commercial Maker

During the second week, the students are given an opportunity to take the point of view of the persuader by considering how they would make their own commercials. On the first day of this unit, a handful of candy is scattered on a table and students are asked to develop a TV commercial that would entice viewers to buy this particular kind of candy. They're also provided with questions to consider while making the commercial of their choice (see Exhibit 11.1, at the end of this chapter) and a model storyboard (see Exhibit 11.2, at the end of this chapter). This encourages them to think about what feelings an advertiser wants the viewer to have, and to pay closer attention to the devices advertisers use to evoke these feelings.

The objective of this exercise is to teach students that the story a commercial tells and the way the maker tells it can have a powerful effect on the viewer. Working in teams over the next week, they develop a number of "stories" designed to play upon the feelings and desires of viewers—in this case their peers—in order to persuade them to buy the product. One particularly ambitious group decides to focus on two aspects of what they define as "competition": the desire to do well and the wish to be popular and admired. They create a story concept that says, "Candy makes you smarter," and in the little skit they write and present to the class, the boy who eats candy has more energy and therefore can pay attention in class rather than dozing off. He also studies better and is more cheerful with his friends.

Because it involves active participation rather than more passive reflection, this unit works particularly well for the "doers" in the class, although even the shyer ones and the kids who tend to be more intellectual and contemplative seem to have fun with it. Ms. Obrig counts it a resounding success (Box 11.3).

Box 11.3: Ms. Obrig's Reflection

I am so excited! This class was fabulous! I have to admit, I was a little concerned about whether all the kids would be able to get it. I'm relieved that they all seemed actively involved. I was really taken with how easily the students moved to create increasingly manipulative messages in their stories! I have to work hard to make sure that the students realize how vulnerable they can be as recipients of the commercial message, whether on television or in their social life. I am thinking now of using the making of commercials as part of individualized curriculum for students – a homework assignment or class project that teams could work on together, depending on their needs and personal styles. I learn a lot from viewing the different levels of student awareness.

Self-Awareness and Media Literacy

Over the next two weeks, the students critique their commercials (with an emphasis on positive feedback); interview their parents to get their comments on how advertising portrays people; watch and discuss videos that focus on stereotypes in advertising and how they affect one's own ideas about oneself; and share their work with the rest of the school by presenting mini-term projects at a school assembly.[1]

In their final write-up, graduate students Shetal Shah and David Walcyk had this to say about their experience with bringing media literacy into the classroom:

Initial results point to the conclusion that the combination of commercial communication education and social-emotional self-awareness skills development does promote the advancement of critical thinking skills in both understanding the messages of television advertising and in understanding the role that it plays in eliciting your emotions.

At a time when so much of what appears on television and in the other mass media is aimed at convincing us to buy something or to live according to someone else's version of happiness, it's important to help children and adolescents understand what they are feeling and thinking in response to these messages. We are in competition for the hearts and minds of our young people, as we help them to make meaning of what they see. If we encourage students to become more conscious of the form and content of what they are watching and how they are responding to it both consciously and unconsciously, we can help them learn to live in an increasingly media dominated world without being overly distracted or unwittingly seduced by the visions presented to them by advertisers.

To reinforce the opportunity for parents to become involved in their children's TV viewing, we asked the students to discuss their commercial-making projects with their families, and report back these discussions to the class.

Box 11.4: Author Reflection (Robin)

I am glad that the kids "got it" – that they understood the difference between what they were thinking and feeling, and what the commercial makers wanted them to think and feel. I am grateful to have had the opportunity to work with these children. I am awed by their creativity and imagination. I believe this has made a real difference for the kids in terms of looking at commercials (and all media, for that matter) in a more critical and analytical way. I am aware that our conscious efforts to teach "as a team" had a positive impact on the emotional climate in the classroom, and fostered creativity. I was aware of stepping back at times to make room for others. I am glad I did!

Exhibit 11.1

Commercial Class Worksheet

Please answer the following questions for each commercial that we view.

1. What details did you notice the most?

2. Give a brief description of the ad.

3. Who is the target audience for this commercial? Parents? Children? Teens?

4. What is going on in the commercial? What story is being told?

5. What is the message being sent to the audience?

6. Does the message work? List what you remember about the message. What are your thoughts? List details that the message communicated, or that interfered with the message being successfully communicated to the audience.

7. What feelings is the commercial's creator trying to elicit from the audience?

8. Is he/she successful? Did you experience those feelings while watching the commercial?

9. What are the values portrayed in the commercial?

10. What are the specific opportunities for critical thinking?

11. Do you want to buy the product or service?

Exhibit 11.2   Storyboard for Commercial

Storyboard for Commercial

12
Meet A Master Teacher

Mrs. Hall is a master teacher. She has a passion for motivating students. She understands that she must unlock both their rational and emotional brains in order for them to excel in school. She has developed the ability to reflect on and identify the qualities that may unlock a student's learning potential, and strategies that enable her students to experience these qualities for themselves. She is confident enough to recognize what she doesn't know about her students, and finds ways to enlist their help in seeking those answers. She stays aware of her own feelings and uses them to guide her actions, and she encourages her students to be aware of and manage their own feelings as an important part of learning.

We want to give you the opportunity to observe Mrs. Hall in action as she implements many of the skills we have been presenting throughout the book. Therefore, in this chapter, we share how this teacher uses her own self-awareness to utilize her own emotional information, and develop teaching and learning strategies that meet the learning needs of individual students.

Meeting A New Class

It's 9AM on the first day of school. Students walk down the hall sharing summer stories. Teachers smile at one another in a knowing way. Classrooms are set-up. In her 20 years as a teacher, Sarah Hall has entered first-day classrooms from first through twelfth grade. Yet she hasn't lost the feelings of anticipation and anxiety that she always experiences when meeting a class for the first time. Today she enters a sixth grade class and gazes at the eager (and not so eager) faces before her. How will the personality of this class and each of its students come to life?

Mrs. Hall is aware of her emotional information, and makes sense of her moment-to-moment experience of feelings, physical body sensations and emotional memories. For example, she knows that she is feeling both nervous and excited; she also recognizes that her stomach is tightening, which usually happens just before 9AM, the time the first class begins. Walking past other teachers on the hallway, she notices that she is now more relaxed; and realizes that when other teachers look relaxed, she often feels less stressed.

Over time, Mrs. Hall has learned to observe emotional information about herself and her students as a source of data with which to guide her work. To do this, she has developed her self-awareness skills. She has learned to acknowledge her feelings before setting them aside for later consideration. This approach has helped her to become a more effective teacher and greatly reduced both her self-criticism and the stress it creates on herself and her students.

Reflecting on the Class

As the class comes to order, Mrs. Hall is mindful of her feelings of anxiety and excitement. Experience has taught her that such feelings often give her the emotional information to better understand the class and herself. When she was a new teacher and the class acted in an unruly way, she often assumed that *she* was doing something wrong. For example, whenever a student acted strangely in class, Mrs. Hall assumed she wasn't giving clear directions and restated her words. Now she understands that the student's behavior may be totally unrelated to what's going on in the classroom.

Mrs. Hall also pays careful attention to her *self-talk*, the silent dialogue within herself through which she considers her thoughts and feelings. Let's listen in on her self-talk as Mrs. Hall looks out at her class.

Box 12.1: Mrs. Hall's Self-Reflection

Will this be a group of serious learners, or of procrastinators and comics? I hope this is not a group of live wires like two years ago. They could never settle down in one place for more than three minutes! Maybe it will be like the quiet group of third graders who always waited for me to pull the information out of them. Now slow down, Sarah, this isn't totally about you. It's about them, too. Don't be so quick to judge. Reign in your first impressions, and allow each student to enter the class with a fresh slate. The personalities will make themselves known soon enough. Just slowly encounter each child and acknowledge that you know they are here.

The room feels upbeat. Mrs. Hall makes eye contact with each student, raises her voice slightly, and says, "Good morning! My name is

Mrs. Hall. I'm happy to be here this year. I see several of you who I already know: Sally, Phil, David. I'm looking forward to teaching all of you this year."

Mrs. Hall talks with the students about plans for the week. At least four students in the class are eager to discuss their summer readings, but a number of their classmates avoid her eye. Although she suspects that the summer readings were not widely appreciated, Mrs. Hall continues to encourage class discussion. As the conversation progresses, her attention is continually drawn to three students: Susan, Antoine, and John.

Over the next three weeks, Mrs. Hall continues to be drawn to these three students. She wonders not only about these students, but also what it is about herself that draws her attention toward them. From her years of experience, she is confident that her own feelings about these children will provide her with emotional information. For example, she remembers a third grader named Renatta who was thought by other teachers to have a learning disorder exhibited through inattention. Mrs. Hall's emotional information took her in a different direction. Her personal response to Renatta coupled with observation of Renatta's social and emotional skills, led Mrs. Hall to the conclusion that Renatta was inattentive due to a lack of competency in self-calming skills, which she quickly helped Renatta to develop. As a result, instances of Renatta's inattention quickly decreased.

Most teachers are sensitive to and aware of their students' needs. Although students often believe they are lost in the sea of faces in the classroom, teachers actually notice many details of a student's individual behavior in class. Mrs. Hall is keenly aware of each student's behavior and she uses these observations together with her emotional information regarding each student to develop objective hypotheses to effectively facilitate student learning. For example, is she really just responding to a student's actions in a given moment, or do certain student behaviors trigger strong feelings and reactions that relate to her own prior experiences? Is her strong response to a student actually a sign that she needs to address an unspoken student need? Mrs. Hall will consider questions like these to make sense of her emotional information about Susan, Antoine, and John.

Understanding Susan

Susan is a petite, brown-eyed sixth grader who sits in class as quietly as a mouse. She certainly is not a discipline problem, and she doesn't disturb any other students. Nevertheless, she captures Mrs. Hall's interest and attention because she appears to drift in and out of class. Susan sometimes makes eye contact with Mrs. Hall, but more often she concentrates on doodling on her notepaper. She will drop her pen or pencil on the floor a few times during class and then bend over to pick it up. She slouches in her chair and appears to be terribly bored.

After several of Susan's pencil-dropping incidents, Mrs. Hall begins to feel annoyed and is about to speak to Susan, when suddenly Susan raises her hand and offers a brilliant insight about the discussion. Susan perceives something in the summer reading that nobody else has noticed—not even Mrs. Hall. Yet after sharing this one extraordinary comment, Susan returns to her fog and appears to disconnect from the class.

Turning her self-awareness into emotional information, Mrs. Hall reminds herself that when she is both pushed by a student's distracted behavior and pulled by the child's talents, she knows that she needs to pay close attention to understanding her own strong reactions as well as close attention to the student.

Mrs. Hall wants to express appreciation to Susan after class, to encourage her to continue sharing her thoughts, but her feelings tell her to give Susan space. When Mrs. Hall approaches Susan with positive words, the child appears timid and surprised. "It wasn't anything," she says. "In fact, I noticed lots of things about the characters in the story. So much so that I got confused. I had more I wanted to say about the story in class, but there are so many things I noticed that I just couldn't get it all into words fast enough. It's really tiring. I'm not very good at English."

Before Mrs. Hall can respond, Susan averts her eyes and walks away. Mrs. Hall wonders why Susan seems so timid and distracted. Is she a physically based learner who feels stress when not physically engaged in learning? Is there a problem that Susan is worried about that is causing her distraction? Mrs. Hall needs to understand more, and she resolves to find a time to talk in greater depth with Susan. For now, she'll try to gather more information about her student.

Susan has been at this school since kindergarten, so her file is full of records. Her report cards show a distinct pattern of distracted behavior and inconsistent performance—her grades range between A+ and C+. Since kindergarten, teachers have recognized the power of Susan's intellectual abilities: she can do challenging math problems and pick up a nuance in the reading that other students do not see. But, her efforts are not sustained, and Susan is often noted as missing homework, not paying attention in class, and continuously underachieving. Her second grade and fourth grade teachers thought the distractibility might be related to an underlying learning disability, but the school's learning specialist found no clear evidence of any such problem.

Mrs. Hall is intrigued by the combination of Susan's giftedness and distractedness; she is a child with an obvious talent who has not yet learned to unleash it. Susan sends out occasional signals that something special is going on inside her mind. But then she goes back into her own world, doodling and dropping the occasional pencil on the floor. Mrs. Hall wonders if she will join the list of teachers who have been baffled by this child's behavior. To help Susan improve her academic performance, Mrs. Hall has a number of ideas for learning strategies that could increase Susan's self-awareness:

- If Susan understood her own style of learning, she might be able to identify the social or emotional skills she needs to better manage her own learning process.
- Developing confidence in her oral communication skills might help Susan more effectively ask her peers or teachers for help with her schoolwork when she needs it.
- Practice of stress relaxation techniques might help Susan focus more comfortably on classroom discussions.
- Susan could explore whether feelings of anxiety are blocking her from expressing herself in classroom activities. For example, when Susan is distracted, Mrs. Hall would like her to begin to notice what she is thinking about and journal about it. In this way Susan can become skilled at self-monitoring and eventually managing her own reactions.

Mrs. Hall knows what a missed opportunity it would be to let a gifted child like Susan not realize the potential of her abilities. She also knows that students like Susan can easily fall through the cracks by doing just well enough academically and behaviorally not to stand out. Mrs. Hall knows that Susan must pay greater attention to her reactions in order to become self-aware enough to set objectives for changing her own behavior.

Reaching Out to Antoine

Antoine draws Mrs. Hall's attention because of his continuous chatting with students in the northeast corner of the room. While he is never oppositional, he creates a distraction for Mrs. Hall. Antoine is a tall, large boned, muscular boy who is sitting in the right hand side, third seat of the room. His intense presence, including his dark curly hair and large brown eyes are riveting. His deep, burly voice seems to penetrate the class whenever he speaks. Of course, he's quick to put his hand in front of his mouth as he whispers a remark to the boy sitting in front of him.

Mrs. Hall realizes that Antoine's strong physical presence is not his fault, however she is disturbed by his lack of consistent attention and she is angry that he is getting more attention from some of the students than she is. The first two times he interrupts, she handles the situation by sending him a long, serious stare. The stare gets the attention of most students. Antoine, however, seems totally unconcerned about Mrs. Hall's gaze and continues to chat with his friend. Finally, Mrs. Hall looks directly at Antoine and very calmly says, "Antoine, would you see me after class for a few minutes?" She tries not to sound irritated, which might only fuel more attention to Antoine. For the remainder of the class, Antoine appears to be relatively quiet.

Antoine seems to be a magnet for the students around him. The girl sitting next to him seems eager to get his attention. In fact, his emotional energy seems to control the whole northeast corner of the room. While he raises his hand often and contributes some worthwhile observations to class discussion, Antoine has defined his sphere of influence in the northeast corner. Mrs. Hall knows she needs to break up this "corner club" quickly, or she could lose control of the class.

After class, Mrs. Hall pulls Antoine aside and mentions that she has noticed his talkative nature in class. She asks him to please resist talking to his neighbors so frequently in future classes. Antoine responds cooperatively. "Sorry, Mrs. Hall. It's just I get bored doing the same thing for too long and each point makes me think of something I need to share with my friends. I didn't realize I was disturbing you. I'll try harder."

Mrs. Hall thanks him for his cooperation and says that she looks forward to having him in class. Within herself, she is worried that Antoine could become more of a problem. She reminds herself not to be controlled by her own discomfort or reactions that lead her to feel that Antoine is a troublemaker. She makes a mental note to think more deeply about the feelings that Antoine's behavior triggers in her.

Mrs. Hall is sure to pick up Antoine's school file. From the comments of other teachers on past report cards, she learns that Antoine is a popular boy with his classmates, a successful athlete, and an average student with a B/C grade range. His standardized test scores reveal that he has good potential for learning—on aptitude tests he scores in the 85 percent and above range. He also is performing at least on grade level in all his subjects.

Antoine has not been recognized as a serious discipline problem, but he leaves a trail of incidents that form a pattern of a child who demands the attention of teachers. In kindergarten, for example, he was banned from the block pile for two weeks after using the marbles from the Chinese Checker set as ammunition for the toy cannon that he built with Lego pieces. In fifth grade he was associated with a group of boys who were rowdy enough on the basketball court during break that they were required to spend the last six weeks of school in daily detention. Antoine was clearly a major influence within the group.

Mrs. Hall is struck by three thoughts in reading Antoine's file. First, she realizes that she needs to get the class under her control quickly, and that she would like to enlist Antoine's cooperation. Second, she wonders if there is some way to help Antoine learn how to manage his pattern of distraction more effectively, so that it doesn't get in the way of his academic performance. She believes he has too much potential to be performing at an average level. In addition, the work this year will be harder, and his classroom distractions will only weaken his performance further. Third, Mrs. Hall is concerned that the pattern of distracted behavior could progress to more self-destructive behavior as Antoine enters his teenage years.

Mrs. Hall has a number of ideas for emotional learning strategies that she would like Antoine to explore this year. These strategies might allow him to use his obvious social skills in the service of his academic performance. For example:

- Antoine needs to become self-aware of the role of emotion and temperament in his learning process. For example, he may be an emotionally-based learner who learns most effectively through interaction with others.
- Antoine could work on improving his self-regulation skills in both recognizing his feelings and in finding ways to channel them in support of his learning.
- Because he seems to be a natural leader, Antoine could be paired with a student like Susan to help her to develop confidence in her communication skills.
- Antoine could use a journal to develop greater awareness of his influence on others. He could then discuss his journal notes every week with Mrs. Hall.

When the students prepare contracts with Mrs. Hall detailing what social and emotional skills they will focus on developing this year to increase their learning effectiveness, Mrs. Hall plans to ensure that Antoine has a full set of objectives to keep him busy.

Seeking John

John catches Mrs. Hall's attention because of the totally blank expression on his face. His body may be in her class, but his mind seems to be in a different world. He is polite and answers questions when called upon, and he does not create any problems in the classroom, yet there is something in his gaze that is riveting to Mrs. Hall. He appears too somber for a 12-year-old boy.

Mrs. Hall is aware that she feels uncharacteristically angry with John for no apparent reason. Listening to her emotional information, she realizes that this is how she used to feel as a child at the breakfast table, watching her brother stare into space. She will observe her feelings more closely to separate out what feelings belong to her history, and which are being stirred up by John's behavior. Mrs. Hall understands that emotionally John is bringing out her protective instincts, and she wonders why. Perhaps it is because he reminds her of Ramon, a very bright student she knew several years ago. Ramon went off to an Ivy League school and ended up suddenly dropping out for no apparent reason. Something about John triggers the same feelings in Mrs. Hall as the ones she had toward Ramon, and she knows she has to be careful not to project on John unfairly. Instead, she will cautiously observe and try to understand her reactions toward him.

When Mrs. Hall asks John about what he is doing when he sits and stares into space in class, he responds: "Well, I think about the discussion. If I don't have a point to make, I don't speak. Is there something wrong with that?"

Mrs. Hall mentions that the class is going to be doing a team project shortly, and that she will be interested in the role John chooses to contribute to his team. She tells him that it's important to be an active contributor as well as an active listener.

When Mrs. Hall checks John's file, she finds a history of good grades and high test scores; in fact, he is always one of the top students in the class. There is never a mention of any problems, although his parents report that he doesn't seem interested in any friends. He discovered computers in kindergarten, and spends most of his time playing computer games, reading, and building models at home. John's mother made him join their church group, but other than that he just doesn't seem to be drawn to people.

Every report card since kindergarten encourages John to participate more in class. His teachers recognize that he is bright and does well, but all want him to speak up in class. Since this message has recurred for six years now, it is clear that John has not chosen to act on it.

Of course, Mrs. Hall appreciates children who are naturally introverted, and she does not believe that being quiet is necessarily a problem. John would clearly not be targeted as a problem student by any of the counselors or other teachers in the school. But Mrs. Hall wants to understand him better, and to understand how he sees his way of relating to others in the class. The curriculum requires group work and several team projects, and Mrs. Hall fears that John may not learn effectively in these situations.

Mrs. Hall has several potential ideas for learning strategies that could foster self-awareness for John. He could benefit from identifying the strengths and weaknesses of his social and emotional skills. Mrs. Hall guesses that his strength is self-regulation and that his growth area would be in connection to others.

- Perhaps working on project assignments with Antoine would provide John with a model for developing relationships, or perhaps John could lead the project team of an appropriate group of students.
- John might explore writing creative poetry as a means to express his feelings and further his self-awareness.
- He might also benefit by keeping a journal about his observations of the reactions of other students in the class. By discussing these observations with Mrs. Hall, John could express his attentiveness to the interpersonal dynamics of the class—another means to raise his awareness. In addition, this approach would give Mrs. Hall a chance to understand John's perspective of the classroom.

Mrs. Hall will explain to John that she will include attention to these behaviors as part of John's letter grade in class.

Recognizing the Need for Emotional Learning

After two decades of teaching, Mrs. Hall still has a passion for the profession because she strives to make a difference in students' lives. She is committed to reaching all of her students. Self-awareness and emotional learning help her to better understand what drives learning behaviors. They also help her teach her students to better recognize and develop their own capabilities. Mrs. Hall often finds that she has hunches and feelings about each student's potential. She knows she can use her own experience and emotional awareness to test these hypothetical approaches, and in turn help her students test their own capabilities for themselves. The major requirement, though, is that all students gain greater and more accurate self-perception. They need to be trained to use their own emotional information effectively.

Figure 12.1, (at the end of this chapter), represents the information that self-aware teachers like Mrs. Hall use to develop social and emotional strategies for effective learning. Mrs. Hall considers her own awareness of her thoughts and emotional information along with those of individual students when formulating the underlying components of each strategy. Mrs. Hall also needs to consider her self-awareness and her perception of individual students when deciding how to objectively review her own emotional information. Finally, she finds it useful to consider, whenever possible, the shared thoughts and emotional information of parents and other teachers. The convergence of all this data helps to both test and integrate emotional information with other people's thoughts when creating strategies.

Teachers often tell us that they are so busy focusing on the needs of their students that they forget to pay attention to the important contribution that their own emotional information can make to their professional growth. In order to take adequate care of herself, Mrs. Hall needs to be self-aware. As Mrs. Hall has become skilled at emotional self-awareness, she has a clearer strategy for how to develop herself as well as her students. To support this personal development goal, she sets emotional learning goals for herself:

- Regarding Susan, Mrs. Hall needs to work on tolerating her own discomfort when Susan swings from distracted to engaged.
- Regarding Antoine, she needs to separate her natural impulse to control him from her understanding that his behavior may be a sign of some other need.
- Regarding John, she needs to remember that her own feelings of anger toward him may have as much to do with her own history as with his behavior.

The greater self-awareness that Mrs. Hall can develop for herself, the more she notices several things happening in her life as a teacher:

- She gains flexibility in understanding the learning needs of her students and developing more effective and individualized, emotional learning strategies.
- She understands where she is carrying stress and releases it.
- She is able to manage the classroom through less heavy-handed discipline and more subtle cues to the class, which makes the entire classroom experience more effective for both students and teacher.

Exhibit 12.1

Information the Self-Aware Teacher Uses to Develop Effective Emotional Learning Strategies

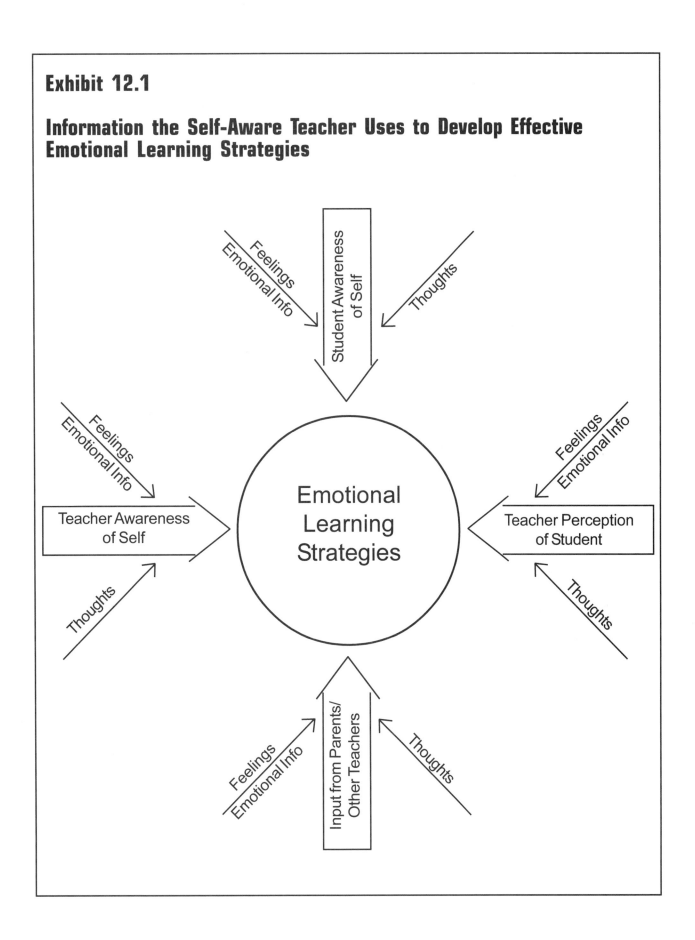

13
Developing Self-Aware Teachers

As we experienced in Chapter 12, Mrs. Hall uses her self-knowledge to help motivate and educate her students. Thanks to the continuous professional and personal growth that comes from turning her attention inward, she is better able to understand her reactions to her students and where these reactions may be rooted. By using self-awareness as a teaching and learning tool, Mrs. Hall is able to help her students engage a fuller range of learning capacities. This is key to helping students demonstrate higher levels of academic performance.

In this chapter, we want to recognize that our first goal in professional development is to enable teachers to educate both the thinking and feeling parts of their students—to develop both the cognitive and emotional brain. Since most of today's teachers were educated before the emotional brain was discovered and understood, professional development programs are needed to train teachers about the important potential contribution to academic performance of self-awareness and social-emotional learning, and how to provide related classroom instruction.

Our second goal in professional development is to move a school from handling issues on a reactive basis to having teachers in place who draw on a system-wide approach to differentiating social and emotional learning. This approach, addressing social and emotional learning, must be well integrated into the curriculum and activities of the school. Many times a school is facing a series of recent problems that have an emotional component such as bullying or name-calling. The professional development session for teachers can, therefore, start from a specific and then move to the context of the larger school curriculum.

Throughout this book, we have presented the programs and models that we have turned to in developing our own self-awareness and building our students' skills. We have identified a range of frameworks for viewing distinctions between students that are the basis of differentiated learning strategies. All of the lessons can also provide a rich experience in self-awareness and emotional learning for the reader. Exhibit 13-1, (found at the end of this chapter), provides an overview of the goals and objectives that teachers specifically need to master to understand and effectively teach these lessons. Take some time to practice them for yourself, not simply because doing so will help you in the classroom, but because you deserve the benefits of the experience.

Making Links through Experiential Training

The intellectual link between self-awareness, self-management ability, and effective learning is obvious to most teachers. For example, teachers understand that students cannot learn if they are distracted, preoccupied by a fight on the playground, worried about problems at home, or hungry. Teachers also recognize that students tend to retreat from group work if they fear ridicule or if their peers ostracize them. What is not always so obvious is the way in which these same concepts naturally apply to teachers themselves. Some teachers we meet are at first uncomfortable with the idea that their own self-exploration is central to effective teaching.

Many of the group trainings we conduct are experiential, using films, videos, or literature to serve as a starting point for applying our understandings of our own feelings and thoughts to classroom situations. Our goal is to help teachers gain access to their own emotional information so they can understand how this information influences their role as a teacher before they try to teach this lesson to their students.

One of our case studies, for example, includes the movie *Mrs. Doubtfire*, which deals with children's view of their parents' divorce. After teachers view a clip from the movie, we turn the discussion to how they might have feelings that would influence the way they treat a child whose parents are divorcing. In the course of the discussion, some teachers realize that their unconscious feelings about divorce often guide how they treat a child whose parents are divorcing.

For example, if a teacher "feels" parents give up interest in their child during a divorce, she may not call them into a conference and instead begin to deal with the child alone. If a teacher "feels" that mothers are most responsible for children in divorce, she may call only the mom about a student's classroom behavior. Or, perhaps the dad will be the focus of a teacher's attention because she believes that fathers too often get left out of their children's lives when parents split up.

The outcome of the discussion is not our focus. What we want teachers to grasp is how feelings they may not consciously be in touch with directly influence their behavior. Once they become self-aware of these feelings, they have the direct emotional information upon which to make conscious choices of how to act. Thus for teachers, building self-awareness is a continuous process of becoming more familiar with the "inner teacher," the one who is really in charge of their classroom.

Implementing Professional Development in Elementary School

As we write, we are working with Community School District #2 in New York City implement a new professional development program for elementary grades focused on social- emotional learning. The program, called Project EXSEL, aims to change school culture by transforming the relationship between guidance counselors and teachers, by enabling guidance counselors to spend part of their time helping teachers bring social-emotional learning into classroom curriculum. A critical piece of this program is professional development in the area of emotional awareness, offered through trainings conducted over the duration of the three-year project.

The kick-off event for the professional development program took place at the Children's Museum of Manhattan, with participating teachers and guidance counselors involved attending to view the museum's newly opened Peanuts Exhibit. Jointly sponsored by the museum and Educators for Social Responsibility, the exhibit focuses on the different feelings, personal dilemmas and conflicts that children face. It invites participants to develop emotionally intelligent solutions, and sets a wonderful example for educators to follow in integrating social and emotional learning into the school curriculum. (For those teachers who do not have access to rich resources like this museum, we recommend working with students to create your own exhibit in art class or with toys from home. Kids will get enthusiastic about the project. Parents and other teachers love seeing what the kids create, which can be a social and emotional learning experience unto itself!)

Playing with Charlie Brown and Friends

Life-sized characters and kid-size interactive stations are scattered about the museum floor to encourage children, teachers and parents to step into Schultz's fictional neighborhood. Each of the galleries focuses on a particular theme, which is reflected in its cartoon strips, displays, and stations. Special labels provide targeted information to assist adults in facilitating children's learning and play. "Think about your favorite Peanuts character. Why do you find that character so engaging? Think about your own life and experiences. How would you feel in the situations depicted throughout the exhibit? How would you handle these situations?"

Visitors are invited to walk onto the baseball diamond so familiar to Peanuts fans, meet Charlie Brown, Linus, and Lucy, and join their game. Toss a ball into the glove of the outfielders, and wait for that solid congratulatory message when you succeed!

The second gallery, "Peanuts Park", invites you to lose yourself in the power of imagination. Visit Snoopy's doghouse, where you can dress up and pretend you are any one of the Peanuts characters. Woodstock's nest allows kids you to build a home that is safe and secure. The nest is a place to think about how terrific bedtime can be for sharing thoughts, worries, and dreams.

In the third gallery, "You're Not Alone, Charlie Brown," you can learn about communication and the impact of positive and negative words as you listen to taped interviews with children and participate in interactive stations. Send Snoopy "Flying Ace" messages to help steer his plane over a mountain range. Choose words of encouragement and watch Snoopy soar! But if you select put-downs and criticisms, the plane sinks with negative comments.

Explore your feelings. Deal with frustration as the kite-eating tree steals your kite. Take a turn in Lucy's psychiatrist's booth, where you pick a situation card and think about how the characters on the card feel. Try to put yourself in their shoes. Adults, too, have a lesson to learn: What messages of encouragement or discouragement are you sending kids, either in your communication with them or in the interactions that they observe you having with others?

Our hope that this would be fun, instructive, and transferable to the classroom was confirmed by teachers who viewed the exhibit. Reflections offered in their sharing groups included the following:

- "Peanuts has always been an important source of humor and comfort for me," said one second-grade teacher. "The exhibit reminded me that these cartoons can be very effective in the classroom for teaching a variety of social and emotional topics."
- "I was particularly touched by the effect of words on Snoopy's success or failure in flying his plane," a kindergarten teacher volunteered. "I remember how important words of encouragement were to me when I was a kid. I'm inspired to use this concept in my classroom."
- In the same vein, a third-grade teacher who was particularly moved by the exhibit added, "I remember how important feeling special was for me. I'd like to encourage my students to understand and appreciate what is special and unique about each and every one of them."

At this point the group as a whole understands what it means to be self-aware, to connect to oneself in a self-reflective way, and to make these feelings explicit. The next step is to give the participants the intellectual framework for understanding self-awareness skills. Together, we talk through the five main competencies that Goleman outlined in *Emotional Intelligence* (1995).

Next, the teachers work in groups to translate some of Goleman's ideas into social--emotional learning for the classroom. The teachers work collaboratively and then share with the whole group the results of their brainstorming sessions. One group comes up with the idea of making their own cartoons to demonstrate all kinds of social and emotional classroom situations. Another group decides that the exhibit is inspiration for an entire wall of words, including some "put-ups" and some put-downs. A third group likes the idea of talking as a class about the feelings of each character, perhaps starting with Charlie Brown and then introducing additional characters.

All in all, we had a terrific time thinking together and working on translating emotional intelligence into classroom exercises. We also had fun reflecting on our own experiences and determining how to take what we have learned back into our classrooms.

At this writing, Project EXSEL is in its third year of implementation. The project has had many successes and many challenges. Successes include:

- Development of over 100 lessons by teachers in the district, incorporating social-emotional learning into the curriculum;
- Development of a video and a website to disseminate the project learnings and lessons;
- Using the new material to train children, who are more emotionally literate;
- Touching the minds and hearts of many teachers who have embraced this learning and are making concrete changes in their classroom.

Challenges include:

- Lack of adequate funds for personnel;
- Continuous work to get the various administrators into active, school-wide support for the program:
- Finding time for professional development—however, teachers tell us that connecting with themselves and listening to their emotional information during the day makes a real difference in their quality of life in the classroom.

Box 13.1: Author Reflection (Robin)

Project EXSEL is two and a half years young! We have had successes and challenges. Personally, I am inspired by the enthusiasm of the project counselors and many others involved, and I am disappointed and frustrated by the logistical constraints that make it difficult for the project to be fully integrated into the schools. I am encouraged at different times, by promises of opportunities to come, then disappointed again when they don't. I feel connected to a committed group of administrators, counselors and teachers who are working for a more successful implementation of the program. Leaders of this project, including myself, have made some mistakes in prioritization, coordination and delegation and have learned from those mistakes. The project is better for this learning.

I do not know yet what the long-term result of this project will be. Most probably, it will be that teachers whose awareness has been raised about the benefits of SEL in schools will take personal responsibility in their classrooms and in their schools for carrying the torch, and will seek further programming. For my part, I will continue to work towards integration and school-wide acceptance. In fact, we are coming up on a long overdue dinner for the principals to explore ways to make the most of the program and discuss where to go next.

Implementing Professional Development in Middle and High Schools

For teachers in grades six through twelve, professional development will take place in a different context as they help students deal with the complex problems of defining themselves in relationship to their peers, schools, communities and future life choices. We often view films, available from most video rental stores, such as *The Breakfast Club* or *The Emperor's Club*, which portray adolescents coping with their feelings in a range of constructive and destructive ways.

Consider an example of viewing *The Breakfast Club*, which portrays a group of students serving a Saturday detention. We ask teachers to identify which of the students they would find most difficult to deal with. Some people say they dislike the popular prom queen character because she reminds them of someone they didn't like in high school. Others identify with her because she reminds them of someone they wished would like them in high school, but didn't. As the discussion continues, some of the teachers realize that the reason a student seems difficult is often found within the teacher's life experience, not just in the student's behavior. Teachers come to realize that their personal feelings, attitudes, and beliefs play a critical role in helping them be fully present— or absent—from the leadership of the classroom.

Continuing to discuss the movie in the context of differentiated teaching and learning strategies, we explore frameworks, competency building and teaching methods that respond to the observed emotional needs and skills required by one character versus another. We discuss which students are particularly difficult for a teacher to handle, and ways colleagues have found that work with that type of student.

Depending of the objectives of a school and its faculty, we include a number of topics in a two hour, half day or full day professional development program. These include:

- Understanding the meaning of emotional information;
- Defining ways self-awareness is implicitly taught in the existing curriculum and how to make those lessons explicit, using the SOURCE model discussed in Chapter 2;
- Teaching basic skills in the health curriculum that can be reinforced throughout the other parts of the curriculum;
- Understanding ways to observe differences in how students experience emotion while learning;
- Approaching stress management in a practical way.

Any chapter of this book, in fact, can provide a focus for professional development.

Box 13.2: Author Reflection (Claudia)

Too often, issues related to emotional learning in middle school or high school are topics where teachers primarily feel inexperienced, exposed and at risk: A student who acts out in class is draining and stress-producing for a teacher; a student who acts out with peers can be dangerous to other students.

These professional development days are not only fun, but can be reassuring to teachers. My experience is that teachers begin to appreciate the wealth of knowledge that comes not only from "the experts," but also from their colleagues, who have developed very effective strategies for teaching about emotion to different types of learners. Unfortunately, with the crunch of school activities, teachers just don't get the time to share their positive experiences in dealing effectively with emotional learning issues. It's only when the crisis of a school shooting or bullying event occurs that schools stop long enough to examine the underlying issues. My hope is that schools and teachers will take the time to re-examine their experiences and curriculums and begin to track in advance the impact of emotion on learning in all areas of the school.

Exhibit 13.1

Objectives for Professional Development of Teachers

Major Professional Development Goals	Specific Objectives	Chapter References
Understand and teach the explicit meaning of self awareness—with emphasis on emotional awareness	Define the role of the emotional brain in learning Define self-awareness Define emotional information	Chapter 1 Chapters 1 & 2 Chapter 6
Understand differences in the role emotion plays for different students while learning—and for different teachers while teaching	Understand differences in human dynamics Understand differences in intensity of feelings during learning	Chapter 3 Chapter 4
Be able to teach a range of skills and frameworks that enable students to understand emotional learning differences and develop targeted skills for competency building	Understand social problem solving skills Understand differences in patterns of stress Understand innersense Understand peer feedback	Chapter 5 Chapter 7 Chapter 8 Chapter 9
Be comfortable teaching these lessons through a range of different methods	Teach material explicitly in existing lessonIntegrate digital technologyIntegrate print and TV media	Chapter 2 Chapter 10 Chapter 11

14
Roadmap to a Self-Aware School

This chapter provides some general guidelines for organizing a school-wide approach to developing a curriculum across grade levels that reinforces the principles and practices we have introduced throughout the book. We believe this material needs to be viewed in a developmental perspective across all grade levels, academic and special subjects, and activities of the school. We offer some basic organizing steps that may help move this process along with minimum stress, and maximum fun! Of course, no two schools are alike in terms of how they get things done. This roadmap (See exhibit 14.1, at the end of this chapter) gives one approach, but our best suggestion is that you take it and build upon it to make it work for your school and your classrooms.

Establishing Major Objectives

Incorporating self-awareness and emotional learning into a school's learning process can be accomplished through five basic strategic objectives:

- Establishing a school project team to review and develop the school's emotional awareness curriculum and objectives;
- Providing ongoing professional development about self-awareness, and particularly emotional awareness, for teachers, counselors, and parents;
- Identifying the basic emotional awareness skills that will be integrated into the school's curriculum;
- Supporting teachers in integrating emotional awareness into their curriculums on an ongoing basis;—
- Developing a strategic perspective on the school's social and emotional learning system.

A school that is serious about increasing the emotional competency of its students needs to be prepared for a long-term effort. We are suggesting some fundamental changes to the conventional approach to teaching and learning. This requires a dedicated, long-term commitment.

Objective 1: Defining the School's Project Team

The person most often identified as skilled and prepared to coordinate the effort is the school counselor. Most schools have a counselor who is responsible for the social and emotional learning of students. In many cases, the counselor's primary role is to work with a small group of "children in need." A commitment to emotional learning requires shifting the counselor's priorities from serving the troubled few to serving all children. This is by no means a simple task.

Counselors we speak with are already overburdened by their existing responsibilities. However, when a whole school commits to self-awareness and emotional learning, counselors tell us that over time their roles become much more manageable. As classroom teachers learn to practice self-awareness and emotional learning skills, they become better prepared to teach these skills to students, thus lessening the counselor's load. A system-wide focus on social and emotional skills ultimately reduces stress on teacher, counselor, and student.

The senior school counselor, or another teacher who is highly skilled is this arena of knowledge, will serve as the project team leader and will be responsible for reviewing and recommending desired changes to the school's existing social and emotional learning program. The project team leader will direct the health curriculum, incorporate basic self-awareness and emotional learning curriculum into the health program, and help teachers integrate these skills throughout the school's curriculum.

Other members of the project team would include teachers of academic subjects who are highly motivated to understand the role of emotion in the classroom. They also must be willing to pilot modifications to existing curriculum. An outside specialist, too, can be a useful resource for training and consultation in professional development of counselors and teachers.

Objective 2: Providing Professional Development

Professional development is so important that we devoted an entire chapter to it (Chapter 13). However, in the context of project implementation, we must recognize that teachers need to be trained to master the same skills that will be taught to students. Mainly, they need to learn how to access their own emotional information and make decisions about it, as well as understand the role emotion plays in their own learning, teaching and stress management processes.

Professional development programs for parents, taught in the evening or available through the Internet, can complement the professional development training delivered to teachers. As we have stated throughout the book, daily practice of skills is crucial if students are to succeed in nurturing their own learning process. Parents can be a vital force in developing emotional awareness in their children by practicing at home the basic emotional skills that are taught in school.

Objective 3: Identifying Basic Skills

Schools must identify the basic emotional skills that will form the building blocks of their self-awareness and emotional learning program. These skills provide a basic vocabulary upon which to build more advanced skills. The project team can review and recommend well-researched programs of basic emotional skills, some of which have been described in this book.

For emotional awareness skills to be accessible to students in moments of stress, those skills must be overlearned (as we discussed in Chapter 5) and practiced at times of low stress. Only when all members of the faculty "walk the talk" on these skills in exactly the same way do students get to overlearn them. By consistently teaching basic emotional skills, teachers are better able to create a safe and caring environment in which stress can be successfully managed and effective learning can take place. When these skills are practiced again and again and overlearned, they are available to teachers and students at all times. Depending on the nature of the school and the diversity of its student body, the project team will recommend the most appropriate basic emotional skills for its curriculum.

Objective 4: Supporting Teachers

The most effective way to develop student competency in self-awareness and emotional learning is to incorporate the building of these skills into the overall curriculum. There are three basic levels of integration of emotional awareness within the classroom setting.

1) Using a classroom management approach that integrates basic emotional skills.

Particularly in the elementary grades, a teacher can comfortably use any of the basic emotional skills as directions to students in order to manage the classroom. For example, a direction to "Keep Calm" (as we discussed in Chapter 5) will help students settle down and focus on the lesson. When students have overlearned the skill of "Keep Calm," they respond to teacher direction automatically. If a student is unable to "Keep Calm," the teacher can provide the student with additional skill-building assistance, often outside the classroom. What might otherwise become a control and power issue is thus reframed as a straightforward classroom skill-building exercise.

2) Differentiating the classroom to support the role that emotion plays in the learning of different students.

At this level, teachers can help students understand the various ways that personal dynamics, temperament, intensity of feelings, emotional information and stress management influence the learning process of each student (as we discussed in Chapters 3-8). Teachers can help students to both understand the strengths and benefits of their own way of learning, as well as build additional emotional competencies to complement their own natural approach.

3) Making emotional learning objectives integral to the objectives of an existing lesson or module.

In Chapter 2 we explored the SOURCE framework that helps teachers to review areas in their existing curricula that provide natural opportunities for integrating emotional learning opportunities. For example, (as discussed in Chapter 6) a seventh grade math teacher expressed how he had to spend a considerable amount of time in one-on-one extra help sessions overcoming his students' math anxiety before he could address the subject of math. By setting a learning objective for the class to "brainstorm and then contract ways to overcome math anxiety," the teacher defused the anxiety of all students and let the students share in supporting one-another to reach a solution.

Objective 5: Developing a Strategic Perspective

The self-aware school learns to turn its attention to the overall climate, stress, and emotional vitality of the community. Developing a strategic picture of the school's social and emotional learning system provides an opportunity to assess other areas beyond the school's curriculum in which the school may want to extend its commitment to emotional awareness. We recommend looking at a school in terms of seven subsystems, which complement academic learning:

1) Administration

Administration includes the school's mission statement and the way resources are allocated to accomplish that mission. Many schools have a mission statement that reflects a philosophical view toward the education of the "whole child." However, resource allocation does not always reflect this philosophy. A self-aware school will allocate budgets to programs that help integrate self-awareness and emotional learning with other academic activities.

2) Discipline

All schools have some set of rules related to discipline, which usually includes a set of detention, suspension, and probation penalties. With basic emotional skills in place, the school has an opportunity to revisit its discipline policies to incorporate emotional learning. For example, when students demonstrate poor judgment, are they asked to become aware of the emotions that led to the poor judgment and to determine alternative responses? Are they asked to participate in activities that reinforce their learning of alternate ways to handle their feelings so that the poor judgment is not repeated in the future? We believe that both of these activities make sense as a regular part of the discipline system.

For example, at the James Browning Middle School in Connecticut, Principal Jennifer Saloway implemented a "Restitution Policy" where students are asked to make restitution for their poor judgment. In essence, the student must think about the feelings underlying his or her inappropriate actions and the feelings of others affected by his or her behavior, and attempt to make up for them. For example, if a student disrupts a class, he or she is required to create a way to directly address the consequences of his behavior with that classroom teacher in some way, such as assisting in preparing a lesson after school.

3) Counseling
In many schools, the counseling program drives the social-emotional learning program. However, many counselors are focused on solving only the problems of troubled students. In order for all students to develop emotional awareness, the counselor's role must extend into the curriculum and classroom. Unfortunately, it often takes a dramatic event, such as a suicide or violent eruption, for this to happen.

4) Student Activities
Schools should consider whether student activities such as community service programs, assemblies, morning meetings, and clubs express the values and reinforce the skills and beliefs underlying the social and emotional learning program. It is important to philosophically align these activities in a way complementary to the values, skills and principles reinforced in the academic programs.

5) Parent and Community Involvement
Students live and work in the overlapping worlds of school, home, and community. To integrate these influences, we must invite parents and community members into the school as partners. Mailings, meetings and the school website should be used to share information with parents and community. For example, at a small school for early education in Pennsylvania, a forward thinking parent brought together a group of other parents to learn about self-awareness by viewing television commercials. Other schools are building and checking websites to reinforce the school-community linkages.

6) Research and Evaluation

In order to assess the real impact of your self-awareness and emotional learning program on your students and school, you must set up a tracking method. By thinking about what you want to accomplish in advance—be it a change in school culture, behavior, or student performance—you identify the outcomes you want to measure over time. Plans for an appropriate measurement approach should be set up at the outset of your program. Resources for tracking and research do not have to be costly. Sometimes grant money is available to support this work. There are companies, individuals, and universities who can offer advice suited to your particular program needs.

Building the self-aware school requires a depth of commitment, resources, and time on the part of all constituencies of the school population. Becoming self-aware is a major step for a school. Self-awareness can change school culture and enable all students to learn more effectively.

Exhibit 14.2

Roadmap to a Self-Aware School

1) Establish a school project team to review and develop the school's emotional awareness curriculum and objectives.

2) Provide ongoing professional development about emotional awareness training for counselors, teachers, and parents.

3) Identify the basic emotional awareness skills that will be integrated into your school's curriculum.

4) Support teachers in integrating emotional awareness into their curriculums on an ongoing basis:

- Use a classroom management approach that integrates basic emotional skills.
- Differentiate the classroom to support the role that emotion plays in the learning of different students.
- Make emotional learning objectives integral to the objectives of an existing lesson or module.

5) Develop a strategic perspective on the school's social and emotional learning system including: 1) Management; 2) Discipline; 3) Counseling; 4) Parent and Community Involvement; and 5) Research and Evaluation.

15
It All Starts With A Teacher!

The spirit of the Master Teacher is eloquently summed up by Parker Palmer in his thought-provoking book *The Courage to Teach*. The concept of "the teacher within, a voice not of conscience, but of identity and integrity" (Palmer, 1998, p.30) is central to his work, and he offers the following "truths" about the relationship between self-awareness and teaching:

> Education is the attempt to "lead out" from within the self a core of wisdom that has the power to resist falsehood and live in the light of truth . . . compels us to look at two of the most difficult truths about teaching. The first is that what we teach will never "take" unless it connects with the inward, living core of our students' lives, with our students' inward teacher. . . . The second truth is even more daunting: we can speak to the teacher within our students only when we are on speaking terms with the teacher within ourselves.

Palmer reminds us that it is our ability to know ourselves that allows us to connect to the real lives of our students and harness the personal power that we bring to our roles as teachers. We share his vision of teaching, and in this chapter we reach out to the spirit of Mrs. Hall that lives in all teachers.

Committing to Professional Development

Master teachers understand the importance of professional development in stimulating the vitality and energy that comes from continuous curiosity and engagement in the teaching process. We've offered many examples of this engagement in the teachers we've introduced you to throughout the book. We've had the opportunity to share our experiences and our visions. Now it's time to put the focus on **you** as the leader. As you make the commitment to bring these skills into the classroom, you join a growing group of teachers from around the world, who recognize the important role that emotional awareness plays in the learning process of their students. These teachers also know that they must be able to understand and use their own feelings as a guide so that they can model these skills for their students.

Understanding feelings and translating them into emotional information is a critical part of the education process. Rachel Carson explained the important role of feelings in knowledge development:

> I sincerely believe that for the child...it is not half so important to *know* as to *feel*. If facts are the seeds that later produce knowledge and wisdom, then the emotions and the impressions of the senses are the fertile soil in which the seeds must grow. (Cited by Laura Parker Roerden in Lantieri, L. 2001, p. 71)

Brain researchers now confirm Carson's metaphor as accurate: the emotional brain and the cognitive brain do not work in a hierarchy but in a partnership, like fellow musicians in a good orchestra. Effective learning and teaching involves both thoughts and feelings.

Students are certainly aware of their teachers' thoughts and feelings. As New York City guidance counselor Barbara Luque points out:

> What is it about those teachers that everyone loves, that makes them so popular in the first place? Even if they can't put words to it, children are extremely astute at picking up on what you are feeling, and what you are or are not directly communicating. They *know* if teachers are mentally, as well as physically, there with them or not. They *know*, perhaps more than I used to think, about who is making the effort to teach versus those merely going through the motions. They can tell you if you are having a good day or a bad day— serving as both a barometer and a reflection of your state of mind.

Indeed, both a teacher's verbal and non-verbal messages tell a story that is read by students. You can walk in with a smile, greet students by name, and ask them how they are; or you can head straight for your desk, tired or preoccupied with problems, paying half attention to the faces that greet you. Both messages communicate your mood, intended or unintended.

As we work with many teachers around the world in our seminars and presentations, we are excited to meet educational leaders, who are actively and often passionately bringing emotional information into their work. We'd like to share some of the different ways in which they are taking the lead.

Linda Lantieri, a leader in violence prevention, is leading an effort to transform schools into caring and peaceable communities through the implementation of skills that build emotional awareness.

> I believe we need to see schools as active and alive organisms that place the highest value on self-knowledge, healthy interpersonal relationships, and building community. These goals are not incompatible with the pursuit of academic excellence—indeed, they foster it—but without care, respect, and kindness, what purpose does intellectual competence serve? (Lantieri, L. 2001, p. 9)

It's also exciting to see educators, who are early in their careers, with the same passion for building an educational system in which emotional information plays an important role. As Sarah Coste, a recent graduate of the RCCP Master's program at Lesley College, heads off to teach fourth grade in Maryland, she recognizes the integral role that self-awareness and emotional learning will play in her teaching,

> Teaching reading and emotional learning needs to be closely integrated. I have no doubt that by developing the self-awareness and emotional learning skills of my students I will maximize their potential for learning as well as create a safer and more caring learning environment for high achievement.

Lauren Hyman, a young teacher who now serves as Director of Education Programs at the Center for Social and Emotional Education in New York City, reinforces Sarah's belief:

> In my experience, once children are able to identify how they are feeling in a situation, their problem-solving techniques are enhanced and in turn they are better able to learn. Self-awareness diminishes obstacles to learning.

These young educators echo the beliefs of those with long-term experience. Frank Moretti, previously Associate Headmaster of the Dalton School in New York, and now the Executive Director of the Center for New Media, Teaching and Learning at Columbia University sees self-awareness as central to a teacher's responsibility.

There is one thing that every mature teacher knows, and that is that the only variable in the classroom is the teacher. The teacher must always assume that the direction, feeling of community, standards of mutual respect, creation of an atmosphere of risk taking, and the fertile and visible field of human connections that is often the source of individual creativity are the responsibility of the teacher herself. And that the teacher's capacity to respond to the shifting unpredictable circumstances depends largely on her awareness of who she is.

Indeed, we see educators in all parts of the country who are taking the lead in placing emotional learning in a central position in the educational process. There are heads of schools, like Jim Benz, the head of a school in Seattle, who are taking personal responsibility for defining and leading the implementation of the school's social and emotional learning program. There are teachers like Story Leonard, a history teacher from Sante Fe, who see emotional learning as the center of students' educational experience, and encourage other faculty members and administrators to seek professional development in this area.

There are school counselors like counselor Angela Murphy from Florida, who seek to develop the emotional awareness of both parents and students, through parent "out-reach" and student "in-reach." There are leaders in educational research and evaluation like Ted Repa, who are setting the research in place to measure what is really working in social and emotional learning programs.

In other parts of the world, educators are joining together to place self-awareness at the center of the educational process. A group of innovative teachers in Sweden are seeking ways to make understanding the individual "human dynamics" of self-awareness a core feature of their approach to teaching and learning. A superintendent of schools in Israel is requiring all teachers in the Tel Aviv schools to attend "wisdom of the heart" professional development programs. We talk with teachers in Brazil, Malaysia, Mexico, Australia, Japan and a host of other countries that are all recognizing and implementing programs that bring self-awareness and emotional learning to the center stage of social and emotional education.

We have shared the approaches that we have tried, seen in action and experienced. Each of you will have your contributions to make. To bring self-awareness and emotional learning to the center of education in all schools is a long-term effort that will require many hands and many voices.

Now it's time for **your voice** to be heard. It can be heard in the safety of your classroom or in the halls of your school, or in reaching out to others to take the lead in building self-awareness and emotional learning as the center of education. Each of these roles is equally important. It's your choice. But do let **your voice** be heard.

Glossary

Basic skills: Set of essential skills that a school will include in its curriculum to develop self-awareness and emotional learning; examples referred to in the book include Keep Calm, Relax, Temperament Watch, and Know Your Purpose. A school has the choice of selecting the skills that best fit its culture and overall curriculum.

Critical thinking: The use of cognitive skills and strategies, as well as "emotional information," for effective problem-solving and decision-making.

Cognitive brain: In contrast to the emotional brain, the cognitive brain governs such mental operations as perception, judgment, memory, and problem solving.

Conflict resolution: The primary focus of the RCCP program, that incorporates discussing feelings, listening, and cooperation as a problem solving approach as opposed to violence or other aggressive means.

Differentiated classroom: A philosophy of thinking and learning that recognizes individual differences in children's interests, readiness, styles of learning, and experiences, in the approach and management of the classroom.

Emotional awareness: The process of focusing on our "emotional information" to understand where it comes from and what it means; it can be momentary, or the integration of impressions over time.

Emotional brain: The part of the brain and nervous system that processes emotion, feelings, and bodily sensations.

Emotional information: The moment-to-moment meaning-making of the experience of our feelings, emotions, physical body sensations and emotional memories.

Emotional learning: Incorporating emotional information into the learning process.

Enneagram: A 2500 year old tool that identifies nine basic patterns of individual development, and ways of managing sources of stress and security, that can be used by high school students and teachers.

E-SOURCE: A useful framework for teachers in considering the ways that self- awareness is taught in their curriculum. (emotional information; self-regulation; outlook; uniqueness; resilience; connection; energy)

Facilitative leader: In contrast to the lecturing method of teaching, the *teacher as facilitator* assists students in coming to their own insights and observations through experience in a participative classroom.

Identity: A self-concept, that some believe is transitory and others believe is stable over time, that refers to the essence of who you are.

Innersense: A term used by Claudia Shelton to describe the self-reflection that supports students in visualizing in their minds their own special and unique personal qualities.

Human Dynamics Program: A developmental system that identifies five basic patterns, which describe how different people function and interact with one another.

Know your purpose: A term used by Claudia Shelton to describe the basic self-reflective skill the enables individuals to check not only their objective path to accomplishments, but also their emotional awareness of the process they follow to get there—and the reasons they are going there to begin with.

Media: A format for information and information sharing that can take many different forms (i.e.: print media, television media, new media)

Myers Briggs Type Indicator: The most widely used psychological instrument in the world that identifies differences between people by examining four preferences for how people see and experience the world and how they make decisions.

Neutral mode: A term used to describe the momentary state one experiences during self-awareness in which one is able to perceive feelings, thoughts and actions without judgment

Overlearning: A term used by Linda Bruene that suggests practicing a skill repetitively until it becomes automatic. Overlearning emotional skills makes them accessible under stressful situations.

Reflection: The inner process of turning one's attention towards feelings, thoughts, and behavior related to a person or topic under consideration.

Relax: A basic skill that uses guided imagery to help students calm themselves, get in touch with their inner thoughts, understand feelings and gather emotional information.

Reflective feedback: A process that helps students understand and articulate thoughts and feelings about their reactions to themselves and others; giving them a way to compare their impressions to those of others.

Resilience: An ability to recover from or adjust easily to misfortune and change.

Resolving Conflict Creatively Program (RCCP): A school-based social and emotional learning program grounded in conflict resolution and inter-group relations that has demonstrated success in reducing violence and creating caring learning communities. It is built upon six principles: co-operation, caring communication, appreciation of diversity, appropriate expression of feelings, responsible decision-making, and conflict resolution.

Self-Awareness: The process of focusing on our thoughts and emotional information to understand where they come from and what they mean; it can be momentary, such as understanding a feeling in the moment, or the integration of impressions over time, such as recognizing life purpose.

Self-Aware Classroom: A classroom in which a teacher has reflected on her curriculum, class management process, and role as a teacher to incorporate emotional learning as a central focus.

Self-Aware School: A school in which the administration and faculty has reflected on philosophy, curriculum, management process, and culture, incorporating emotional learning as a central focus.

Self-knowledge: The result of the reflective process, which leads to a more developed and integrated sense of self.

Self-talk: The inner conversation that people have with themselves.

Social-emotional learning: An integrated approach to teaching and learning associated with the social and emotional development of children from pre-school through high school.

Social Problem Solving/Social Decision Making Program: A behaviorally oriented, school based educational program in social and emotional skills development that demonstrates success in facilitating problem solving and decision-making; it includes basic skills such *keep calm, BEST, listening position, and FIGTESPIN.*

Temperament watch: A basic skill fur understanding innate emotional pattern that individuals can recognize in themselves and others.

Bibliography

Banner, R. Study finds programs in schools can curb violence among young. *New York Times,* September 15,1999.

Baron, R. & Wegerle, E. *The Enneagram Made Easy.* San Francisco: Harper San Francisco, 1994.

Comer, J. Social and Emotional Learning and Digital Technology Conference at Teachers College, Columbia University, November 4, 1999.

Cooper, R. K. & Sawaf, A. *Executive EQ.* New York: Perigree, 1996.

Covey, S. R. *The Seven Habits of Highly Effective People.* New York: Fireside, 1989.

Damasio, Antonio R. *The Feeling of What Happens.* New York: Harcourt Brace and Company, 1999.

Elias, M. J. & Bruene-Butler, L. Social Decision-Making and Problem-Solving. In J. Cohen (Ed.), *Educating Hearts and Minds: Social Emotional Learning and the Passage into Adolescence* (p. 87–88). New York: Teachers College Press, 1999.

Elias, M. J. & Tobias, S. E. *Social Problem-Solving.* New York: Guilford Press, 1996.

Elias, M. J., Tobias, S. E., & Friedlander, B. S. *Emotionally Intelligent Parenting.* New York: Harmony Books, 1999.

Elias, M. J., Zins, J. E., Weissberg, R. P., Frey, K. S., Greenberg, M. T., Hayes, N. M., Kessler, R., Schwab-Stone, M. E., & Schriver, T. P. *Promoting Social and Emotional Learning: Guidelines for Educators.* Alexandria, VA: Association for Supervision and Curriculum Development, 1997.

Gardner, H. *Frames of Mind: The Theory of Multiple Intelligence.* New York: Basic Books, 1983.

Goleman, D. *Emotional Intelligence.* New York: Bantam Books, 1995.

Goleman, D. McKee, A & Boyatzis, R. *Primal Leadership: Realizing the Power of Emotional Intelligence.* New York: Harvard Business School Press, 2002.

Kagan, J. *Unstable Ideas: Cognition and Self.* Boston: Harvard University Press, 1989.

Kriedler, W. *Conflict Resolution in Middle School.* Cambridge, MA: Educators for Social Responsibility, 1994.

Lantieri, L. From Punishment to Prevention. *Reclaiming Children and Youth, 6,* 155–159, 1997.

Lantieri, L. *Schools with Spirit.* Boston: Beacon Press, 2001.

Lantieri, L., & Patti, J. The Road to Peace in Our Schools. *Educational Leadership, 54,* 28–31, 1996.

Lantieri, L., & Patti, J. *Waging Peace in Our Schools.* Boston: Beacon Press, 1996.

LeDoux, J. *The Emotional Brain: The Mysterious Underpinnings of Emotional Life.* New York: Simon & Schuster, 1998.

Leider, R. J. *The Power of Purpose.* San Francisco: Berrett-Kohler Publisher, Inc, 1997.

Levine, J. *The Enneagram Intelligences.* Westport, CT: Bergin & Garvey, 1999.

Reuven, B. & Parker, D.A., eds. *The Handbook of Emotional Intelligence.* San Francisco: Jossey Bass, 2000.

Roerden, L. P. Lessons of the Wild. In L. Lantieri (Ed.), *Schools with Spirit.* Boston: Beacon Press, 2001.

Riso, D. R. *Discovering Your Personality Type.* New York: Houghton Mifflin Company, 1995.

Seagal, S. & Horne, D. *Human Dynamics: A New Framework for Understanding People and Realizing the Potential in our Organizations.* Waltham, MA: Pegasus Communication, 1997.

Seagal, S. & Horne, D. *Human Dynamics in Children's Park Design: Fundamental Distinctions in Children's Problem Solving, Learning and Development* [Videotape]. Los Angeles, CA, 1990.

Seligman, M. E. P. *The Optimistic Child.* New York: Houghton Mifflin Company, 1995.

Shelton, C. M. "How Innersense Builds Commonsense". *Educational Leadership, 57,* 61–64, 1999.

Shelton, C. M. "Portraits in Emotional Awareness". *Educational Leadership, 58,30-32, 2000.*

Stern, R. "Columbine's challenge: A call to pay attention to our students". *Voices from the Middle, 7,* 34–36, 1999.

Stern, R. & Rosenzweig, D. "Hormone driven kids: A call for social and emotional learning in the middle school years". *Voices from the Middle, 7,* 3–8, 1999.

Stern, R. *Social and Emotional Learning: What Is It? How Can We Use It to Help our Children?* aboutourkids.org, posted 12/5/00.

Sylwester, R. In search of the roots of adolescent aggression. *Educational Leadership, 57,* 65–69, 1999.

Tomlinson, C. *The Differentiated Classroom: Responding to the Needs of All Learners.* Alexandria: VA: Association for Supervision and Curriculum Development, 1999.

Tomlinson, C. A. Reconcilable differences. *Educational Leadership, 58, 2000.*

Villani, S. Impact of Media on Children and Adolescents: A 10-year review of research. *Journal of American Academy of Child and Adolescent Psychiatry, 40,* 392–401, 2001.

Weissberg, R.P., Caplan, L., Bennetto, M. and Jackson, A.S. *The New Haven Social Problem-Solving Module.* Chicago: University of Illinois at Chicago, 1990.

Resources

Available from National Professional Resources, Inc.
(Print & Video)

Abourjilie, Charlie. *Developing Character For Classroom Success.* Chapel Hill, NC: Character Development Publishing, 2000.

Armstrong, Thomas. *7 Kinds of Smart: Identifying and Developing Your Many Intelligences, Revised.* New York, NY: Plume (The Penguin Group), 1999.

Armstrong, Thomas. *Beyond the ADD Myth: Classroom Strategies and Techniques* (Video). Port Chester, NY: National Professional Resources, Inc., 1996.

Armstrong, Thomas. *Multiple Intelligences: Discovering the Giftedness in All* (Video). Port Chester, NY: National Professional Resources, Inc., 1997.

Armstrong, Thomas. *Multiple Intelligences in the Classroom, 2nd Edition.* Alexandria, VA: ASCD Publications, 2000.

Beane, Allan L. The Bully Free Classroom: *Over 100 Tips and Strategies for Teachers K-8.* Minneapolis, MN: Free Spirit Publishing, 1999.

Begun, Ruth W. *Ready-to-Use Social Skills Lesson (4 levels: Pre K-K; 1-3; 4-6; 7-12)* West Nyack, NY: Center for Applied Research, 1995.

Bernardo, Rudy, et al. *Building Character Schoolwide: Creating a Caring Community in Your School.* Chapel Hill, NC Character Development Publishing, 2000.

Bocchino, Rob. *Emotional Literacy: To be a Different Kind of Smart.* Thousand Oaks, CA: Corwin Press, 1999.

Cohen, Jonathan (editor). *Educating Hearts and Minds: Social Emotional Learning and the Passage into Adolescence.* New York, NY: Teachers College Press, 1999.

Coles, Robert. *Moral Intelligence of Children.* New York, NY: Random House, Inc.,1997.

DeRoche, Edward F. & Williams, Mary M. *Educating Hearts & Minds.* Thousand Oaks, CA: Corwin Press, 1998.

Dotson, Anne C., & Dotson, Karen D. *Teaching Character/Teacher's Guide.* Chapel Hill, NC: Character Development Publishing, 1997.

Elias, Maurice. *Raising Emotionally Intelligent Teenagers: Parenting with Love, Laughter and Limits.* New York, NY: Three Rivers Press, 1999.

Elias, Maurice, et al. *Promoting Social-Emotional Learning: Guidelines for Educators.* Alexandria, VA: ASCD, 1997.

Elias, Maurice, & Tobias, Steven. *Social Problem Solving: Interventions in the Schools.* New York, NY: Guilford Press, 1996.

Etzioni, Amit. *New Golden Rule: Community & Morality.* New York, NY: Basic Books, 1996.

Feldman-Barrett, L., & Salovey, P. (Eds.). *The Wisdom in Feeling: Psychological Processes in Emotional Intelligence.* New York, NY: Guilford Press, 2002.

Gardner, Howard. *Frames of Mind: The Theory of Multiple Intelligences* (10th Anniversary Edition). New York, NY: Basic Books, 1993.

Gardner, Howard. *How Are Kids Smart? Multiple Intelligences in the Classroom* (Video). Port Chester, NY: National Professional Resources, Inc., 1995.

Gardner, Howard. *Intelligence Reframed.* New York, NY: Basic Books, 1999.

Gardner, Howard. *Multiple Intelligences: The Theory in Practice.* New York, NY: Basic Books, 1992.

Gardner, Howard. *The Disciplined Mind.* New York, NY: Basic Books, 2000.

Gardner, Howard. *The Unschooled Mind: How Children Think and How Schools Should Teach.* New York, NY: Basic Books, 1991.

Gerzon, R. *Finding Serenity in the Age of Anxiety.* New York, NY: Bantam Books, 1998.

Glasser, William. *Choice Theory: A New Psychology of Personal Freedom.* New York, NY: HarperCollins, 1998.

Glasser, William. *Reality Therapy in Action.* New York, NY: HarperCollins, 2000.

Glasser, William. *The Quality School: Managing Students Without Coercion, 2nd Edition.* New York, NY: HarperCollins, 1998.

Glenn, H. Stephen, *Raising Self-Reliant Children in a Self-Indulgent World.* Orem, UT: Empowering People, 1989.

Goleman, Daniel. *Emotional Intelligence: A New Vision for Educators* (Video). Port Chester, NY: National Professional Resources, Inc., 1996.

Goleman, Daniel. *Emotional Intelligence: Why it Matters More Than IQ.* New York, NY: Bantam Books, 1995.

Gregory, Gale and Chapman, Carolyn. *Differentiated Instructional Strategies: One Size Doesn't Fit All.* Thousand Oaks, CA: Corwin Press, 2002.

Hanson, Helene and Iervolino, Constance. *Differentiated Instruction Practice Video Series: A Focus on Inclusion (Tape 1), A Focus on the Gifted (Tape 2).* Port Chester, NY: National Professional Resources, Inc. 2003.

Hart, Leslie. *Human Brain and Human Learning.* Kent, WA: Books for Educators, 1998.

Heacox, Diane. *Differentiated Instruction: How to Reach and Teach All Learners (Grades 3-12).* Minneapolis, MN: Free Spirit Press, 2002.

Healy, Jane M. *Failure to Connect.* New York, NY: Simon & Schuster, 1998.

Jensen, Eric. *Brain-Based Learning, Revised.* San Diego, CA: The Brain Store, 2000.

Jensen, Eric. *Successful Applications of Brain-Based Learning* (Two video set). Port Chester, NY: National Professional Resources, Inc., 2000.

Josephson, Michael & & Hanson, Wes. *Power of Character: Prominent Americans Talk About Life, Family, Work, Values & More.* San Francisco, CA: Jossey-Bass, 1998.

Kagan, Spencer. *Building Character Through Cooperative Learning* (Video). National Professional Resources, Inc., 1999.

Kohn, Alfie. *Punished by Rewards.* New York, NY: Houghton Mifflin, 1993.

Kohn, Alfie. *The Schools Our Children Deserve.* New York, NY: Houghton Mifflin, 1999.

Krovetz, Martin L. *Fostering Resiliency: Expecting All Students to Use Their Minds and Hearts Well.* Thousand Oaks, CA: Corwin Press, 1999.

LeDoux, Joseph. *The Emotional Brain.* New York, NY: Simon & Schuster, 1996.

Levine, Mel. *A Mind at a Time.* New York, NY: Simon & Schuster, 2002.

Levine, Mel. *Developing Minds Multimedia Library (Videos).* Boston, MA: WGBH, 2001.

Lewis, Barbara A. *What Do You Stand For? A Kid's Guide to Building Character.* Minneapolis, MN: Free Spirit Publishing, 1997.

Lewis, Catherine, et al. *Eleven Principles of Effective Character Education* (Video).National Professional Resources, Inc., 1997.

Lickona, Thomas et al. *Character Education: Restoring Respect & Responsibility in Our Schools* (Video). National Professional Resources, Inc., 1996.

Lickona, Thomas. *Educating for Character: How our Schools can Teach Respect & Responsibility.* New York, NY: Bantam Books, 1992.

Lickona, Thomas. *Raising Good Children.* New York, NY: Bantam Books, 1994.

Macan, Lynn, et al. *Character Education: Application in the Classroom, Elementary Edition* (Video). National Professional Resources, Inc., 1998.

Mayer, J.D., Salovey, P. and Caruso, D. *Emotional intelligence as Zeitgeist, as personality, and as a mental ability.* In R. Bar-On and J.D.A. Parker (Eds.) *The Handbook of Emotional Intelligence* (pp. 92-117). San Francisco, CA: Jossey-Bass, 2000.

Mayer, J.D., Salovey, P. and Caruso, D. *Models of emotional intelligence.* In R.J. Sternberg (Ed.), *The Handbook of Intelligence* (pp.396-420). New York, NY: Cambridge University Press, 2000.

Mayer, J.D., Caruso, D. and Salovey, P. *Selecting a measure of emotional intelligence: The case for ability scales.* In R. Bar-On and J.D.A. Parker (Eds.) *The Handbook of Emotional Intelligence* (pp.320-342). San Francisco, CA: Jossey-Bass, 2000.

Mayer, J.D., Salovey, P. and Caruso, D. *The Mayer-Salovey-Caruso Emotional Intelligence Test (MSCEIT).* Toronto, ON: MultiHealth Systems, 2001.

Nelson, Jane. *Positive Discipline.* Orem, UT: Empowering People, 1996.

Pert, Candace. *Emotion: Gatekeeper to Performance* (Video). Port Chester, NY: National Professional Resources, Inc., 1999.

Pert, Candace. *Molecules of Emotion.* New York, NY: Scribner, 1997.

Ryan, Devin A. & Bohlin, Karen E. *Building Character in Schools.* San Francisco, CA:Jossey-Bass, 1998.

Salovey, P., & Sluyter, D. (Eds.). *Emotional Development and Emotional Intelligence: Implications for Educators.* New York, NY: Basic Books, 1997.

Salovey, Peter et al. *Optimizing Intelligences: Thinking, Emotion & Creativity* (Video). National Professional Resources, Inc., 1998.

Sergiovanni, Thomas J. *Moral Leadership: Getting to the Heart of School Improvement.* San Francisco, CA: Jossey-Bass, 1992.

Shaw, M. A. Your Anxious Child: *Raising a Healthy Child in a Frightening World.* New York, NY: Birch Lane Press, 1995.

Stirling, Diane, Archibald, Georgia, McKay, Linda & Berg, Shelley. *Character Education Connections for School, Home and Community.* Port Chester, NY: National Professional Resources, Inc., 2002.

Teele, Sue. *Rainbows of Intelligence: Exploring How Students Learn.* Thousand Oaks, CA: Corwin Press, 1999.

Teele, Sue. *Rainbows of Intelligence: Raising Student Performance Through Multiple Intelligences* (Video). Port Chester, NY: National Professional Resources, Inc., 2000.

Tomlinson, Carol Ann. *How to Differentiate Instruction in Mixed-Ability Classroooms, 2nd Edition.* Alexandria, VA: ASCD, 2001.

Vincent, Philip F. *Promising Practices in Character Education: Nine Success Stories from Across the Country, Volume II.* Chapel Hill, NC: Character Development Publishing, 1999.

Wolfe, Patricia. *Brain Matters: Translating Research into Classroom Practice.* Alexandria, VA: ASCD, 2001.

Order from:
National Professional Resources, Inc.
25 South Regent Street
Port Chester, NY 10573
1-800-453-7461/914-937-8879
www.nprinc.com

About the Authors

Claudia Marshall Shelton

As a teacher, school counselor, administrator and leadership development specialist, Claudia Marshall Shelton has developed and implemented school-wide strategies and curriculum focused on self-awareness and emotional learning that affect student academic performance, teacher satisfaction, school climate, and parent involvement in school life. Currently President of the Hopewell Company, which provides professional development, parent programs, and leadership development for schools and businesses throughout the country, Claudia regularly publishes articles, keynotes speeches and conducts training programs at universities including Columbia University, Teachers College and City University of New York. She holds M.A., M.B.A., and M.Ed. degrees and is a licensed and nationally certified professional counselor.

Robin Stern

As an educator, psychotherapist, and psychological consultant, Robin Stern has developed and implemented programs to promote personal and professional growth through self-awareness in schools and businesses. She is adjunct associate professor at Teachers College, Columbia University, and a Director of both The Woodhull Institute for Ethical Leadership, and Educators for Social Responsibility. Robin teaches and consults about social-emotional learning and digital technologies, as well as the psychology of leadership and the development of emotional competence. She also writes and speaks about ethical leadership and emotional intelligence, social-emotional development, and communication. She holds an M.A., and a Ph.D. in psychology.

DATE DUE

GAYLORD   PRINTED IN U.S.A.